Working with Child Abuse
Social Work Practice and the Child Abuse System

Working with Child Abuse

Social Work Practice and the Child Abuse System

BRIAN CORBY

Open University Press

Milton Keynes · Philadelphia

Open University Press
Celtic Court
22 Ballmoor
Buckingham MK18 1XW

and

1900 Frost Road, Suite 101
Bristol, PA 19007, USA

First Published 1987   Reprinted 1990

British Library Cataloguing in Publication Data
Corby Brian
  Working with child abuse: social work
  practice and the child abuse system.
  1. Child abuse
  I. Title
  362.7′044   HV713

  ISBN 0-335-15396-8

  ISBN 0-335-15395-X Pbk

Library of Congress Cataloging in Publication Data
Main entry under title:
Corby, Brian.
  Working with child abuse
  Includes index.
  1. Child abuse—Great Britain—Prevention.
2. Child abuse—Great Britain—Investigation.
I. Title.
HV751.A6C67 1987 362.7′044   87-16503

ISBN 0-335-15396-8

ISBN 0-335-15395-X (Pbk)

Text design by Clarke Williams

Typeset by Gilbert Composing Services, Leighton Buzzard, Beds.
Printed in Great Britain by St. Edmundsbury Press, Bury St. Edmunds, Suffolk.

Contents

Acknowledgements

There are many people who helped considerably in the writing of this book. They include the social workers from the districts in which the fieldwork was carried out and the parents who admitted me to their homes and were prepared to talk to me about personal and painful subjects. In particular I would like to thank the principal social workers (child abuse) in North City who were enthusiastic and confident enough to give me access to all aspects of the system which they managed.

Two colleagues at Liverpool University, Chris Mills and Howard Parker, have been particularly supportive and helpful, and I am grateful to the university for granting me time to complete and write up my research. I should also thank colleagues in the Sub-department of Social Work Studies for standing in for me during this time. Finally I would like to thank Linda Deeringer for typing the bulk of the manuscript.

Introduction

On any conceivable version of the events under inquiry the death of Jasmine Beckford on 5 July 1984 was both a predictable and preventible homicide. (The report of the inquiry into the circumstances surrounding the death of Jasmine Beckford, p. 287).

1985 was a crisis year for those working in the field of child abuse, particularly social workers. With almost sickening regularity the newspapers reported the deaths of young children at the hands of their parents or caretakers in circumstances where social services department and other agency workers were already aware that the children were at some risk.[1] Yearly statistics may prove that in fact 1985 was not an exceptional year for such deaths.[2] Nevertheless their impact will remain and, without doubt, the inquiry report into the death of one of these children, Jasmine Beckford[3], will have considerable influence on policy and practice in the field of child abuse and direct effect on families suspected of abusing their children and on the professionals (particularly those in the front-line) who work with them.

The study described in this book focuses on the day-to-day practice of local authority social workers in the field of child abuse. Research for the study commenced in 1981 at a relatively quiet period as far as recent child abuse history is concerned. The preceding seven years had seen a series of public inquiries into the deaths of abused children[4] and the establishment of a new system and set of procedures[5] for assessing and dealing with incidents of child abuse. To some extent these measures had provided security for those working in this field, and a degree of routinization in what had previously been seen as a high risk area of work. However, by the time the study was completed (in 1985), as has just been pointed out, child abuse had again been highlighted as a major social problem.

At the time of writing there is much concern as to the future of social work practice in the field of child abuse and child care work in general. The Beckford inquiry report is highly critical of the practice in that case and generally criticizes social workers for addressing the needs of families as a whole to the detriment of those of individual children. A recent D.H.S.S. research report[6] describes the present situation regarding social work practice with general child care problems as 'disturbing and depressing'. There is little doubt that changes in practice will result in the near future.[7] While this focus on child care practice is to be welcomed, (there is a pressing need to constantly monitor practice in this field) nevertheless, it is important to ensure that changes are carefully thought out and not hurriedly adopted in response to the public mood or other such factors.

The intention of this study of social work practice in the field of child abuse is to provide further data on the subject and to contribute to any changes in policy and practice that may result from the experiences of 1985. While there is a wealth of research into the aetiology of child abuse[8] and methods of treatment[9] and a good deal has been written about systems for dealing with the problem[10], there has been little direct study of how child abuse work is handled particularly by the statutory agencies.[11] The major exception to this is the work of Dingwall *et al.*[12] which is a case study of how various agencies detect, investigate and initially process child abuse cases. Their research looked at how the practices and ideologies of health and social work professionals combined to define abuse and how abuse cases were processed up to and including the stage of care proceedings. The study to be described in this book focuses on social work practice and includes consideration of ongoing work with families after the early stages of intervention.

It is all too easy to criticize professional practice and to recommend changes in approach. This study does have criticisms to offer, particularly of the systems which act as the framework for practice. It is also critical of certain aspects of social work practice for instance, the covert and rather indirect form of monitoring of families that takes place. Nevertheless it is important to bear in mind the complexity of the issues involved in child abuse work and the pressures and anxieties that surround it. Social workers have to draw a sometimes impossibly fine line between protecting children and re-specting the rights of families to be self-determining. The difficulty of working meaningfully with a family where children are thought to be at risk, but whose parents constantly deny that anything is amiss, cannot be overstated. The pressure created by the publicity which child abuse work has received over the past 12 years leads ultimately to defensiveness and cynicism on the part of practitioners and does not necessarily sharpen their senses. While, therefore, recent research and inquiry findings have pointed to the need for changes in practice we desperately need to be more aware of the practical and ethical problems of working with families suspected of child abuse before we can properly advise social workers and others how to conduct themselves in this sphere.

Notes

1. See Appendix 1.
2. See Appendix 2.
3. 'A Child in Trust'. The Report of the Panel of Inquiry into the Circumstances Surrounding the Death of Jasmine Beckford. (1985). London Borough of Brent.
4. Child Abuse: A Study of Inquiry Reports 1973–81. (1982) H.M.S.O.
5. The D.H.S.S. letter (LASSL(80)4) 'Child Abuse: Central Register Systems' was the last of a series of D.H.S.S. circulars beginning in 1970 which provided guidance for the establishment of the current child abuse system. The most important of the others were:-

    1. D.H.S.S. and Home Office (1970) 'Battered Babies'. Letter CMO 2/70.
    2. D.H.S.S. (1972) 'Battered Babies'. LASSL(26)72.
    3. D.H.S.S. (1974) 'Non-Accidental Injury to Children'. Letter. LASSL(74)13.
    4. D.H.S.S. (1976) 'Non-Accidental injury to Children: Area Review Committees'. Letter LASSL(76)2.
    5. D.H.S.S. and Welsh Office. (1978) 'Release of Prisoners convicted of Offences Against Children in the Home'. Letter LAC (78)22.

6. Social Work Decisions in Child Care: Recent Research Findings and their Implications. (1985). H.M.S.O.
7. The D.H.S.S. has recently published the recommendations of a working party to ministers – 'A Review of Child Care Law' (1985). H.M.S.O. which has implications for practice in the child abuse field where there is recourse to law. The D.H.S.S. is also due to publish new guide-lines for child abuse practices.
8. See for example R.S. and C.H. Kempe, (1978), *Child Abuse*, Fontana, for an overview of the 'emotional deficit' theory of child abuse. R.J. Gelles and C.P. Cornell, (1985), *Intimate Violence in Families*, Sage Publications gives a useful account of a 'cultural causation' view. J. Garbarino, (1977), 'The human ecology of child maltreatment', *Journal of Marriage and the Family*, 39(4) pp. 721–735 outlines another approach looking at the key role that network support systems play in child abuse causation.
9. There are a wide range of studies dealing with the treatment of child abuse

based on a variety of theoretical perspectives. For overviews of the literature and range of approaches see C.T. Shorkey, (1979), 'A Review of Methods Used in the Treatment of Abusing Parents', *Social Casework*, (June 1979) pp. 360–367 and also J.S. Wodarski, (1981), 'Treatment of Parents who Abuse their Children: A Literature Review and Implications for Professionals', *Child Abuse & Neglect*, vol. 5, pp. 351–360.

10. See D.N. Jones *et al.* (1979), 'Case Conferences on Child Abuse: The Nottinghamshire Approach', *Child Abuse and Neglect*, vol. 3, pp. 583–590 and C. Hallett and O. Stevenson, (1980), *Child Abuse: Aspects of Interprofessional Cooperation*. Allen and Unwin.

11. There is a wealth of literature relating to the work of the N.S.P.C.C. in Great Britain since the formation of their battered child research unit in 1968 the work of which is most fully described in E. Baher *et al.*, (1976), *At Risk*, N.S.P.C.C. See also J. Pickett, (1976), 'The management of non-accidental injury to children in the city of Manchester', in M. Borland, *Violence in the Family*, Manchester Univ. Press. Recent developments in approaches by the N.S.P.C.C. are to be found in P. Dale, M. Davies, T. Morrison and J. Waters, (1986), *Dangerous Families: Assessment and Treatment of Child Abuse.* Tavistock.

12. R. Dingwall, J. Eekelaar and T. Murray, (1983). *The Protection of Children: State Intervention into Family Life,* Blackwell.

Chapter 1

Child abuse – The context

There is simply no way of escaping the conclusion that the complete elimination of child abuse on all levels of manifestation requires a radical transformation of the prevailing unjust, inegalitarian, irrational, competitive, alienating and hierarchical social order into a just, egalitarian, rational, cooperative, humane and truly democratic, decentralised one. (D. Gil, *Unravelling Child Abuse*, (1975), American Journal of Orthopsychiatry Vol. 45 no. 3 p. 355.)

The similarities between baby battering and other forms of deviant behaviour are striking. Like delinquency and crime in general, baby battering occurs alongside a constellation of other social inadequacies or failure of adaptation rather than in isolation. Battering parents must be properly classified and the natural history of the condition closely observed before we can be confident about treatment measures other than emergency action. (S. Smith, R. Hanson and S. Noble, *Social Aspects of the Battered Baby Syndrome*, (1974), British Journal of Psychiatry no. 125 p. 579)

Child abuse was 'rediscovered' as a social problem in the early 1960s in the U.S.A.[1] The main agents of this 'rediscovery' were Dr. Henry Kempe, a paediatrician from Denver, Colorado, and his associates. Their ideas were adopted in the late 1960s in Great Britain by the N.S.P.C.C.[2] and were prominent in the important period surrounding the report of the inquiry into the death of Maria Colwell[3] when the framework of the present system for dealing with child abuse was formulated.

Child abuse has been institutionalized and, at the least, tolerated in many societies for hundreds of years.[4] Most pre-industrial Western societies gave absolute power to fathers of families over their children. However, with increasing industrialization came a change in family relationships. Donzelot[5], drawing on French social

1

history sources, describes the process by which paternal power has gradually been eroded over the last two centuries and replaced by a focus on the role of the mother. This has been achieved by means of the influence of philanthropic societies, the medical profession and latterly with the aid of psychodynamic thinking. According to Donzelot, the state has by means of these mechanisms gained a subtle but strong foothold in the family and an important indirect means of controlling how it socializes its young. The illusion of the independence of the family is maintained and the state gets the product it requires. Behlmer's history of child abuse work between 1870 and 1910[6] gives a detailed account of the early stages of this process in Great Britain. During this period the social evils of baby-farming, child vagrancy and physical cruelty to children were tackled by the emerging philanthropic societies such as the N.S.P.C.C. and Dr. Barnardo's and to a less extent by the medical profession. At the end of this period with the passing of the Children Act in 1908 the state had assumed the right to remove children from their homes if their parents had been convicted for assaults or other crimes against them, which would have been considered an unthinkable intrusion into family life in 1870.

Between 1910 and the early 1960s, the issue of child abuse as a major problem virtually disappeared in Great Britain. No-one has been fully able to account for this period of quiescence. According to Behlmer 'widespread faith in the N.S.P.C.C.'s ability to enforce protective legislation bred a dangerous complacency'.[7] It may well be, however, that between then and 1945 the issue of child abuse paled into insignificance in the light of two world wars and prolonged economic recession. The immediate post-Second World War period, however, saw considerable concern and activity about deprived children in the care of state institutions and philanthropic societies. The death of Dennis O'Neill at the hands of his foster-father, led to widespread publicity and added to the already growing demand for better services for children in need.[8] The result of all this pressure was the formation of local authority children departments in 1948. However, Packman's account of the development of these departments demonstrates that cruelty to children was not a major preoccupation of child care officers in the 1950s and 1960s.[9] They were more concerned to provide preventive services to families with general child care problems and to improve the quality of substitute care. The focus even of the N.S.P.C.C. at this time was more on general neglect than on cruelty to children specifically.[10]

However, from the late 1960s up to the present time the problem of child abuse has taken firm hold and become a major focus of attention for British social workers. Pfohl in the U.S.A.[11] and Parton[12] in Great Britain have put forward reasons as to why child abuse should have emerged so dramatically as a major social problem at this time. Both emphasize the role of technological development – the work of Caffey and others had demonstrated the usefulness of radiological innovations for detecting physical ill-treatment of children[13] – and both point to the professional aspirations of the then emerging specialism of paediatrics. Parton argued that in Great Britain the N.S.P.C.C., faced with increasing competition from the state social work services for children (soon to merge with health and welfare departments to form larger more influential social services departments) was seeking a more specialist role. Also the political climate in which fears for the future of the family were being expressed was seen to be receptive to the new ideas which were being developed at this time. If we accept Donzelot's theorizing this period saw a major development in increased control of the family by the state with child abuse being one of the means of achieving this.

The Contribution of Henry Kempe

The key agents of this development were undoubtedly Dr. Kempe and his associates. Their clinical work, allied to the findings of the radiologists already referred to, led them to the conclusion that severe physical ill-treatment of young children was a far more common occurrence than had previously been suspected or admitted. Kempe and his associates publicized the problem in a now famous article published in the *Journal of the American Medical Association* in 1962[14], in which the term 'battered child syndrome' was first used. In this and later works Kempe and his colleagues set out their ideas in a strong and compelling way.[15] They argued that psychological factors were the predominant causes of child abuse. Parents who had suffered depriving experiences themselves as children were unlikely to possess the emotional make-up required to adequately parent their own children. Such parents tended to have unrealistic expectations of their children and the inevitable resulting disappointment in these expectations led to frustration and physical abuse. Such abuse was seen as likely to continue and worsen unless some form of intervention took place. Kempe's method of intervention was, first of all, to protect the child and then to focus treatment on the parent. Children were either removed from their parents or received into hospital with them. The parents then received psychotherapeutic treatment usually by means of individual counselling and, if treatment was considered to be successful[16], children and parents were discharged home or reunited if separation had taken place. Follow-up work, usually carried out by social workers, would normally ensue. Kempe argued that this form of intervention was successful in 80 per cent of all cases referred.[17] In the 20 per cent of cases where treatment was unsuccessful, as in the case of severely disturbed or psychotic parents, it was advocated that children should be permanently separated from their parents.

As their work has continued new ideas and approaches have been developed. Despite their main theoretical emphasis on the psychological causation of child abuse, Kempe and his associates do recognise the contribution of stress and poverty. However, they insist that child abuse is basically a classless phenomenon, being causally connected with childhood experiences of being mothered and their treatment focus is almost exclusively concerned with the emotional aspects. They advocate a range of helping activities other than individual psychotherapy i.e. – group therapy, behavioural therapy, family therapy, the use of crisis hotlines, crisis nurseries and play therapy for the abused children. They have placed considerable emphasis on preventive community work in particular focusing on predicting abusive potential at and around the time of birth with, according to them, 75 per cent accuracy.

The British response

These ideas were readily taken up by the N.S.P.C.C. in Great Britain[18] but with some modifications. Whereas Kempe's treatment involved the use of psychotherapists, N.S.P.C.C. workers were qualified social workers and employed ego-supportive casework techniques in the early period and in more recent times a wider range of methods including family therapy.[19] The N.S.P.C.C. have not had their own residential settings to which parents and children could be admitted together. However, they have developed a wide range of play-group and day-centre facilities. The Park Hospital at Oxford[20] has been the most faithful follower of the approach advocated by Kempe. Here joint residential facilities are provided for children and families along with psychotherapeutic counselling, groupwork, play facilities and therapy for children. In addition staff of this hospital have played a major role in developing community-based resources with particular emphasis on monitoring maternity wards with a view to organizing preventive services.[21] However, it should be stressed that this response to child abuse is the exception rather than the rule. Generally health service provision for families where child abuse is suspected has not developed along the lines suggested by Kempe and his associates though their theoretical ideas lie at the core of paediatric practice in this field.

The main protagonist in the field of child abuse since 1974 has been the local authority social services department. In the period immediately preceding that in which the N.S.P.C.C. in particular was adopting the ideas of <u>Kempe</u> in the way described above, statutory social work services were undergoing major organizational changes that resulted in the creation of unified social services departments in 1971.[22] The emphasis in training and practice in social work was shifting to the application of general skills and principles which could be used in any area of activity and with any client group. In many areas individual social workers were allocated mixed caseloads consisting of a wide range of client groups and types of problems. It has since been argued that this response was a result of misinterpretation of the Seebohm report's recommendations.[23] Whatever the case, the ensuing period was one of chaos and confusion as practitioners and managers grappled with areas of work with which they were largely unfamiliar.[24] As a consequence many of the developments which were taking place at this time in the field of child abuse went unrecognized.

All this changed as a result of the publication of the Maria Colwell inquiry report. This document highlighted the lack of inter-professional coordination and communication which was manifest in this particular case. It also served to sensitize social services departments to the existence of physical abuse of children and to the extent of public indignation felt about it. The result was a swift reaction on the part of the Department of Health and Social Security which by means of a series of circulars issued between 1974 and 1976 established the framework of the administrative system for detecting, investigating and processing child abuse cases that currently exists. The main features of this system were, and still are, as follows –

1. Area Review Committees (A.R.C.'s) drawn from the higher levels of relevant health and welfare agenies whose function is to institute policy decisions and to oversee their general implementation.

2. Case Conference Systems consisting of front-line practitioners from relevant agencies brought together to assess and make decisions about individual cases.

3. Child Abuse Registers for recording the names of children deemed at risk of abuse or further abuse. The main aim of these registers is to ensure that previous instances of officially recorded abuse are not overlooked.

4. Child Abuse Manuals issued by the A.R.C.'s providing guidelines for the various relevant agencies to follow in the event of allegations of child abuse.

This official response was almost entirely a 'managerial' one. There is little doubt that the 'battered child syndrome' as described by Kempe and his associates provided much of the theoretical underpinning to this approach, but their ideas regarding therapeutic intervention were not developed at all. The focus was exclusively on how to recognize child abuse and manage cases with particular emphasis on ensuring good interprofessional communication. No advice was given as to the type and extent of resources to be initiated and developed; implicitly reliance was to be placed on the currently existing health and welfare resources.

Although the basic philosophy and administrative structure have remained roughly the same since 1976 there have been some developments. Following further inquiries into child abuse cases[26] there have been legal and procedural changes with regard to adults with criminal records for offences against children and their right to live in the same household as children.[27] The definition of child abuse has been broadened – as a result of the 1980 D.H.S.S. circular emotional abuse and physical neglect have been added to the list of categories eligible for registration.[28] The 1980s has seen an upsurge of interest in the phenomenon of sexual abuse of children within families[29] and although it is not an official category for registration it is in practice considered as such in many parts of the country.

The current situation, therefore, is that in Great Britain we have a largely 'managerial' response to child abuse administered mainly by the statutory social work agencies. There is little official focus on therapeutic work, though the growth of day centres for families and children in the past five or so years may have provided an indirect therapeutic input. The work of the N.S.P.C.C. has placed more stress on therapeutic intervention and it is currently embarking on a major expansion of resource centres.[30] The experiences of 1985 and criticisms of the child abuse system from various quarters before that[31], however, point to the continuing existence of considerable dissatisfaction with its operation.

Other theoretical perspectives on child abuse

In the remainder of this chapter consideration will be given to the main theoretical controversies in the field of child abuse. Much attention has already been given to the work of Henry Kempe because of its direct influence on the development of British social work practice in this field. It is not surprising that his ideas have been so influential. As has been pointed out by Parton[32], this emphasis on the main cause of abuse being a product of parents' own deprived childhood experiences fitted well with theories of cyclical deprivation which were in vogue in official circles in the early 1970s.[33] Also at this time British social work training was still heavily influenced by psychodynamic thinking.[34] For instance, Bowlby's theory of maternal deprivation was a major influence on social work practice[35], though it had not, before Kempe, been explicitly linked to child mistreatment. Therefore, although Kempe's ideas, particularly with regard to therapy, have not been widely adopted, nevertheless they have contributed greatly to thinking about, understanding and predicting the likelihood of child abuse to a much greater extent than other theoretical approaches.

Yet, particularly in the U.S.A., where far more funding has been allocated to research into child abuse, other theories have been developed and a much broader range of perspectives has been in evidence.

For instance, Gil's study of reported physical abuse of children conducted in the late 1960s[36] placed far greater emphasis on material and social factors in relation to child abuse than did the work of Kempe and his associates. Drawing from a national sample of 1380 cases of abuse reported between 1967 and 1968 Gil found that most of his subjects were from poor backgrounds. Only half of the fathers had been employed throughout the year; nearly a third of the children lived in homes without a father or father substitute; over a third were in receipt of public assistance relief at the time of the abusive incident. By and large parents were not as young as earlier studies of physical abuse had suggested and only 14 per cent of the mothers and 7 per cent of the fathers were reported as having been abused themselves as children. Ninety per cent of the injuries had no lasting physical effects and over half the incidents reported were not considered serious. Gil's findings do not negate those of Kempe – he does not deny the contribution of psychological factors to child abuse, but by taking a broad sample of child abuse incidents as reported to public agencies he provides a different perspective. Gil concluded that 'the scope of physical abuse of children resulting in serious injury does not constitute a major social problem, at least in comparison with several more widespread and more serious social problems that undermine the development opportunities of many millions of children in American society, such as poverty, racial discrimination, malnutrition and inadequate provisions for medical care and education.' Thus by looking at a broad sample of child abuse cases Gil widened the parameters of the subject and pointed to major structural changes in society as the means of tackling child abuse.[37]

The connection between poverty and child abuse is also stressed by Pelton.[38] His survey of child abuse studies led him to the conclusion that 'contrary to the myth of classlessness, child abuse and neglect are strongly related to poverty in terms of prevalence and of severity of consequences. This is not to say that abuse and neglect do not occur among other socio-economic classes, or that, when they do occur, they never have severe consequences. However, widespread reports suggesting that abuse and neglect are classless phenomena are unfounded and misleading. The myth of classlessness persists not on the basis of evidence of logic, but because it serves certain professional and political interests.' Again these views do not refute the psychologically-focused explanations of child abuse, but they emphasize other factors more strongly and have different implications for official responses to the problem.

Another perspective developed in the U.S.A. is that focusing on the ecological aspects of child abuse. Garbarino[39] is critical of the predominance of psycho-pathological explanations of child abuse. Much of child abuse, he argues, is not abnormal. 'It seems essential to distinguish between abuse "caused" by sadistic psychopathology (a small proportion of abuse in general but a high proportion of lethal abuse) and the behaviour of "normal" adults'. A good deal of abuse is seen to be a product of social stress and relatively low levels of skill on the part of care-givers. The problem lies not within the individual, according to Garbarino, but in his or her ability to carry out the parenting role and this is in turn seen as linked to performance in other roles and contacts with wider social networks. He states that the two necessary conditions for physical abuse of children are 1) societal sanction of corporal punishment and 2) social isolation resulting either from a lack of social supports or the failure to use whatever supports are available. He cites the findings of Young[40] and Smith *et al.*[41] to back his thesis.

Gelles is also critical of the primacy given to psychological explanations of child abuse in practice and policy.[24] He too finds sociological explanations of abuse more useful, adopting the view that child abuse is a more normal activity than much of the early pioneering work would lead us to think. In a national survey conducted in 1976[43] 1143 parents of children aged between 3 and 17 were asked to report on their own 'conflict tactic techniques' with children. The findings are listed in Table 1.1.

Table 1.1 Frequency of parental violence toward children.
Violent behaviour – Percentages of occurrences in the past year

	once	twice	more than twice	Total	% of occurrences ever reported
Threw something at child	1.3	1.8	2.3	5.4	9.6
Pushed, grabbed or shoved child	4.3	9.0	18.5	31.8	46.4
Slapped or spanked child	5.2	9.4	43.6	58.2	71.0
Kicked, bit, or hit child with fist	0.7	0.8	1.7	3.2	7.7
Hit child with something	1.0	2.6	9.8	13.4	20.0
Beat up child	0.4	0.3	0.6	1.3	4.2
Threatened child with a knife or gun	0.1	0.0	0.0	0.1	2.8
Used a knife or gun on child	0.1	0.0	0.0	0.1	2.9

Using a definition of abusive acts as those which had a high probability of injuring a child it was found that 1.4 million children in the U.S.A. experience such violence each year. Officially reported incidents of abuse, including all forms of neglect, numbered 788,844 in the U.S.A. in 1980. Clearly, therefore, abuse of children is a widespread phenomenon in the U.S.A. a finding which has important implications for how to respond to it. Gelles and

Cornell[44] argue that child abuse should not be seen in isolation from other forms of family violence for example wife- battering and elder abuse, as they term it. Family violence is explained by the fact that those who inflict violence on others within the family can by and large do so with impunity. The response, according to this thesis, should be twofold, to tackle cultural norms and to control abuse by reducing the opportunities for perpetrators to get away with it.

Defining abuse

Just as American research has developed this theoretical diversity with regard to the nature and cause of child abuse, so it has led the way in examining other important issues such as the problems associated with defining abuse. The excellent study by Giovannoni and Becerra[45] looked at the way in which various professionals involved in the field of child abuse and various lay groups rated different types of abuse. The study started from the hypothesis that definitions of child abuse were socially constructed phenomena and that understanding abuse was impossible without understanding how it was defined. The study was carried out in Los Angeles County in the late 1970s. First, four sets of professionals (lawyers, social workers, police and paediatricians) were asked to rate 60 child abuse vignettes covering a wide variety of types and degrees of abuse. The findings were that there was virtually no consensus about the seriousness of the instances of mistreatment. Statistically significant differences were found among these professional groups in all but 9 cases and there was complete agreement in only 12 per cent of the cases. Overall, police and social workers were in most agreement (73 per cent of the time) and they rated the vignettes more seriously than the paediatricians and the lawyers in that order. The researchers found that 'blindness' to abuse was not a psychological problem but a reflection of occupational perspectives and concerns.

Turning to the lay sample, generally they rated instances of abuse more seriously than did the professionals, but ranked cases in roughly the same order. These lay people were divided for analytical purposes into ethnic and class groupings. Three ethnic groups were identified – blacks, Hispanics and whites. Overall, the blacks and Hispanics rated the vignettes more seriously than did the whites. The blacks were more concerned as a group with deficits of care, the Hispanics about more active abuse. Generally, individuals of lower socio-economic status viewed mistreatment as more serious than did those of higher status.

These findings are used as evidence by the authors to press for much greater specificity and precision in defining different types of abuse. The official trend, however, in both the U.S.A. and Great Britain has been in the opposite direction that is to group all forms of abuse together.

The process by which child abuse is defined has been analysed by Gelles.[46] He stresses that the term child abuse is a socially constructed phenomenon and does not exist until certain judges or gatekeepers, who are selected to apply the definition, do so. Given the diversity of views as to what constitutes abuse, as described in Giovannoni and Becerra's study, this is likely to be a highly complex process. Dingwall *et al.*[47] have studied this process in some detail in two local authority areas in Great Britain. Their overall findings are that, contrary to the views of those who see the process as intrusive and authoritarian, differing views and perspectives between professionals and the over-riding philosophy of our liberal–democratic society lead to largely pro-parent outcomes when an issue is in doubt. Whatever the case, there can be little doubt that the processes by which child abuse decisions are reached are of crucial importance to the way in which the problems are tackled.

In general terms, while in the U.S.A., thanks to generous research funding, focus on child abuse is leading to a diversity of perspectives and consideration of a broad range of issues, the same cannot be said to be true of Great Britain. As emphasised before, very little attention has been given to developing resources for treating or helping families where abuse is suspected – the focus has been almost entirely on improving the system for detecting and managing cases and reliance has been placed on existing resources. Similarly there has been little direct research into child abuse work and related issues – to some extent the findings of public inquiries have served this function. It is as if there has been a reluctance to focus on child abuse because it is considered to be too narrow a topic in itself. One of the consequences of this is that we are woefully ignorant about certain aspects of the subject, the most glaring example of this being with regard to the extent of the problem. There are no national statistics on the number of officially recognized cases of child abuse. We have instead to rely on a 10 per cent example drawn up annually by the N.S.P.C.C. for an indication of trends.[48]

Conclusion

This chapter has outlined the context within which child abuse is dealt in Great Britain and the theoretical issues that are currently being debated here and in the U.S.A. While most of the practitioners in this study were unlikely to have been directly aware of all these issues and controversies at this level they were very much affected by the structures within which they were operating and were faced in real life with many of the contradictions and complexities referred to. How they and the families who were the object of their attentions made sense of and coped with these problems is the subject of the remaining chapters.

Notes

1. Child abuse is often described as having been discovered in the early 1960s. This ignores much of the pioneering work done in the second half of the nineteenth century when the existence of child abuse was clearly recognised. See G.K. Behlmer, (1982), *Child Abuse and Moral Reform in England 1870-1908*, Stanford Univ. Press.
2. See E Baher *et al.*, (1976), *At Risk*, N.S.P.C.C.
3. D.H.S.S., (1974), Report of the Committee of Inquiry in to the Care and Supervision Provided in Relation to Maria Colwell. H.M.S.O.
4. See S.X. Radbill, (1968), 'A History of Child Abuse and Infanticide' in R.E. Helfer & C.H. Kempe (eds) *The Battered Child*, Univ. of Chicago. See also L. Eisenberg (1981) 'Cross-Cultural and Historical Perspectives on Child Abuse and Neglect'. *Int. Journal of Child Abuse & Neglect* vol. 5 pp. 229-308.
5. J.P. Donzelot, (1979), *The Policing of Families,* Hutchinson.
6. G.K. Behlmer, (1982), op. cit.
7. G.K. Behlmer, (1982), op. cit. p.226.
8. Report by Sir Walter Monckton K.C.M.G. K.C.V.O. M.C. K.C. on the circumstances which led to the boarding out of Dennis and Terence O'Neill at Bank Farm, Minsterley, and the steps taken to supervise their welfare. cmnd. 6636. (1945). H.M.S.O.
9. J. Packman, (1981), *The Child's Generation*, Blackwell.
10. See N.S.P.C.C. Annual Report 1956. 31 May, 1956.
11. S. Pfohl, (1977), 'The Discovery of Child Abuse,' *Social Problems*, vol. 24. no. 3. pp. 310-323.
12. N. Parton, (1979), 'The Natural History of Child Abuse: A Study in Social Problem Definition.' *British Journal of Social Work* vol. 9 pp. 431-451. N. Parton, (1981), 'Child Abuse, Social Anxiety and Welfare,' *British Journal of Social Work*, vol. 11 pp. 391-414.
13. J. Caffey, (1946), 'Multiple Fractures in the Long Bones of Infants Suffering

from Chronic Subdural Haematoma.' *Amer. Journal of Roentgen rad. Ther.* vol. 56. pp. 163–173.

see also M. Lynch, (1985), 'Child Abuse before Kempe: An Historical Literature Review.' *Child Abuse & Neglect*, vol. 9 pp. 7–15.

14. C.H. Kempe, F.N. Silverman, B.F. Steele, W. Droegemueller and H.K. Silver, (1962), 'The Battered Child Syndrome.' *Journal of the American Medical Assoc*, 181, pp. 17–24. This article is currently reprinted in *Child Abuse & Neglect*, (1985), vol. 9 pp. 143–154.

15. See R.E. Helfer & C.H. Kempe (eds), (1968), op. cit: R.E. Helfer & C.H. Kempe (eds) 1976, *Child Abuse and Neglect, The Family and the Community*, Ballinger: R.S. & C.H. Kempe, (1978), *Child Abuse*. Fontana.

16. The Kempes' view of success is described in pp. 132/3 of R.S. & C.H. Kempe (1978) op. cit. 'The children from 80 % of the families we treat return home, either directly from the hospital or following a period in foster care. These children, in our experience, have never been injured again once we have been able to confirm four objective changes. First, the abusive parent's image of himself must have improved to the point where he has made at least one friend with whom he shares regular and enjoyable experiences, such as bowling. Second, both parents must have found something attractive in their abused child and be able to show it by talking lovingly, hugging or cuddling. Third, both parents must have learned to use lifelines in moments of crisis, so that they telephone their social worker, a friend, a member of Parent's Anonymous, or else take their children to a crisis nursery. Last, weekend reunions with their child in hospital or foster care must become more and more enjoyable, and increasing responsibility must not have strained the family. It is premature to return the child home if these criteria have not been met.'

17. The issue of successful intervention is a problematic one. While the Kempes claim a high success rate, the Park Hospital in Oxford, operating along similar lines, but without the range of facilities available in Denver, claims a much more modest success rate. See M.A. Lynch & J. Roberts, (1982), *The Consequences of Child Abuse*, Academic Press.

18. See E. Baher, (1976), op. cit.

19. See P. Dale, T. Morrison, M. Davies, P. Noyes & W. Roberts, (1983), 'A family-therapy approach to child abuse: countering resistance.' *Journal of Family Therapy*, vol. 5. 117–143. For a further account see P. Dale, M. Davies, T. Morrison & J. Waters, (1986), *Dangerous Families: Assessment and Treatment of Child Abuse*. Tavistock.

20. See M.A. Lynch & C. Ounsted, (1976), 'Residential Therapy – A Place of Safety.' R.E. Helfer & C.H. Kempe (eds) (1976) op. cit.

21. See M.A. Lynch & J. Roberts, (1977), 'Predicting Child Abuse: Signs of Bonding Failure in the Maternity Hospital'. *British Medical Journal*, 1: 624.

22. This was as a result of the passing of the Local Authority Social Services Act 1970 which implemented the main recommendations of the Seebohm Report (Cmnd. 3703 (1968). Report on the Committee on Local Authority and Allied Personal Social Services. H.M.S.O.). For a brief but useful account of this change see C. Hallett, (1982), *The Personal Social Services in Local Government*, Allen and Unwin.

23. For a balanced account and interpretation of the recommendations of the Seebohm Report regarding specialisation see O. Stevenson, (1981), *Specialisation in Social Services Teams,* Allen and Unwin.

24. See C. Satyamurti, (1981), *Occupational Survival,* Blackwell.

25. See note (5) introduction.

26. See note (4) introduction.

27. Following the inquiry into the case of John Auckland, (Report of the Committee of Inquiry into the Provision and Coordination of Services to the Family of John George Auckland, 1975.) the D.H.S.S. recommended that procedures be established to notify social services departments of the release from prison of any prisoner convicted of an offence against children. Also a new section 1(2)bb) was added to the 1969 Children & Young Person's Act establishing the presence or likely presence of a person who has been convicted of an offence against children (as mentioned in schedule 1 of the Children & Young Person's Act 1933) in the same household as any child or young person as being a ground for bringing care proceedings.

28. D.H.S.S., (1980), Child Abuse: Central Register Systems LASSL(80)4. This circular specifies 4 criteria for registration – 1. Physical abuse. 2. physical neglect. 3. failure to thrive and emotional abuse. 4. children in the same household as a person previously involved in child abuse. This circular also gives guidelines concerning the administration of the register.

29. See for instance R. Porter, (ed.), (1984), *Child Sexual Abuse within the Family,* Tavistock.

30. The 1984 Annual Report of the N.S.P.C.C. stated its aim to be to establish 60 child protection teams across England, Wales and Northern Ireland by 1989 following the raising of £12m in its centenary year.

31. Criticism of the child abuse system has been levelled by those who see it as an illiberal and authoritarian response to families in need. (see H. Geach, (1983), 'Child Abuse Registers – Time for a change' in H. Geach and E. Szwed (eds) *Providing Civil Justice for Children,* E. Arnold: N. Parton and T. Thomas (1983), 'Child Abuse and Citizenship' in B. Jordan and N. Parton (eds), *The Political Dimensions of Social Work,* Macmillan: W. Jordan, (1976), *Freedom and the Welfare State,* Routledge and Kegan Paul. Criticism of the child abuse system has also been voiced by those who see it as far too liberal. Such views are rarely articulated in social work literature, but are more likely to be voiced in inquiry reports and by judges in cases where parents are on trial. For instance the Daily Telegraph on 29 March 1985 reported that 'Judge Pigot severely criticised the London Borough of Brent Social Services in whose care Jasmine (Beckford) had been since 1981. Social workers showed a "naivety beyond belief" said the judge. Time and time again they were fobbed off with excuses for not being able to see Jasmine.' For an analysis of press accounts of child abuse cases see N. Parton (1985) *The Politics of Child Abuse,* Macmillan (pp. 85–97).

Dingwall *et al.*, in their book (R. Dingwall, J. Eekelaar & T. Murray, (1983), *The Protection of Children,* Blackwell) have articulated an intermediary position. They argue that the child abuse system is liberally administered, but that such an approach reasonably reflects the current views of our society with regard to achieving a balance between the protection of children and preserving the rights of the family.

32. N. Parton,(1979) & (1981), op. cit.
33. Sir Keith Joseph, (1972), speech to Pre-school Play-groups Association, press release.
34. For a full account see M. Yelloly, (1980), *Social Work Theory and Psychoanalysis*, Van Nostrand Reinhold.
35. J. Bowlby, (1953), *Child Care and the Growth of Love*, Penguin.
36. D. Gil, (1970), *Violence Against Children: Physical Abuse in the United States*, Harvard Univ. Press.
37. See also D. Gil, (1975), 'Unravelling Child Abuse.' *American Journal of Orthopsychiatry*, vol. 45 no. 3 pp. 346-356.
38. L.H. Pelton, (1978), 'Child Abuse and Neglect: The Myth of Classlessness.' *American Journal of Orthopsychiatry*, vol. 48 no. 4 pp. 608-617.
39. J. Garbarino, (1977), 'The Human Ecology of Child Mistreatment' *Journal of Marriage & the Family*. vol 39 no. 4 pp. 721-735.
40. L. Young, (1964), *Wednesday's Child: A Study of Child Abuse and Neglect*, Mcgraw-Hill.
41. S. Smith, R. Hanson & S. Noble, 'Social Aspects of the Battered Baby Syndrome,' *British Journal of Psychiatry*, vol. 125 pp. 568-582.
42. R. Gelles, (1973), 'Child Abuse as Psychopathology: A sociological critique and reformulation.' *American Journal of Orthopsychiatry*, vol. 43 pp. 611-621.
43. M. Strauss, R. Gelles & K. Steinmetz, (1980), *Behind Closed Doors: Violence in the American Family*, Anchor Press.
44. R. Gelles & C.P.Cornell, (1985), *Intimate Violence in Families*, Sage.
45. J.M. Giovannoni & R.M. Becerra, (1979), *Defining Child Abuse*, Free Press.
46. R. Gelles, (1975), 'The Social Construction of Child Abuse,' *American Journal of Orthopsychiatry*, vol. 45 pp. 363-371.
47. R. Dingwall *et al.*, (1983), op. cit.
48. S. Creighton, (1984), *Trends in Child Abuse*, N.S.P.C.C.

Chapter 2

The Research Issues

The previous chapter considered some of the broader influences on the field of child abuse work. In this chapter attention will be focused first on some of the issues directly relevant to social work practice and policy implementation and then move on to describe the area in which the study took place and the methods of investigation employed.

Social Work and Social Control

Social workers dealing with child abuse are very much acting as agents of social control or regulation as the authors of a recent study rephrased it.[1] From one perspective social workers are agents of social control in everything they do – the control is not necessarily overt and can take the form of being very helpful and acting in the interest of the clients. However, in the field of child abuse, where statutory duties are in force to protect children, social workers have to adopt more overtly authoritarian measures of intervention.

Making use of authority has long been a very difficult problem for social work practitioners. Particularly since the formation of the children's department in 1948 when social work professionalism began to take firm hold in Great Britain,[2] the notion of service of the client has been the dominant hall-mark of the professional ideology. Much of the mainstream literature regarding social work methods and ethics gives little attention to the social control aspects of the work of social services agencies. Client–self-determination has been a major guiding principle of practice.[3] Biestek[4] defined this principle as

16

the practical recognition of the right and needs of clients to freedom in making their own choices and decisions in the casework process. Caseworkers have a corresponding duty to respect that right, recognize that need, stimulate and help to activate that potential for self-direction by helping the client to see and use the available and appropriate resources of the community and his own personality. *The client's right to self-determination, however, is limited by the client's capacity for positive and constructive decision-making, by the framework of civil and moral law and by the function of the agency.*

In this last sentence some recognition is given to constraints on the principle of self-determination, but rather understates the dilemmas for practice. Such a principle is of use in voluntaristic relationships to ensure that clients do not become too dependent and that social workers do not abuse the imbalance of power that exists between them and their clients. However, the exercise of statutorily defined authority of the kind granted to social workers in the field of child abuse raises considerably more difficulties, not least because of emphasis placed on principles such as self-determination in other areas of their work.

Various writers have stressed that help can be constructively offered in relationships where authority rests with one participant.[5] Such writers take a basically consensual view of society and see the soft authority approach as being preferable to more overt use of authority. From this point of view the mainstream practices of social work (i.e. casework and family therapy) are not incompatible with the use of statutory authority. Raynor[6] argues that choice can be offered within an authority relationship, that the probation officer or social worker can act as someone who sets out the options and the possible consequences and leaves the probationer or client to make an informed decision. Such a viewpoint does not see care and control as incompatible. Other writers, however, those who see society more in conflict terms, have argued that such care/control fusion is morally unacceptable and practically difficult to operate.[7]

Social Work Practice and Child Abuse

Turning to the field of child abuse, Parton and Thomas[8] from a conflict perspective, see considerable contradictions and dilemmas placed in the path of social workers. 'It seems to us', they argue, 'that, more than any other issue, child abuse has thrust social workers into the centre of the political arena' (p. 55) 'It is clear that the Maria Colwell inquiry was very much concerned with focusing on and attempting to restructure the relationship between social work, the state and the family and, in the process, with constraining social workers into a more authoritative, directive and more closely monitored form of practice, particularly with certain sectors of the population' (p. 56) 'The way social workers experience their practice in this field is often clouded with fear. Such fear is not simply concerned with the professional anxiety which such situations create, but with a more general fear of being called to account for one's actions' (p. 57). These writers go on to argue that social workers have been deprived of autonomy when working in this field, and that their work is closely monitored by senior managers. Their overall argument is that social workers have been forced to discard a softer more helpful approach to families where children were deemed to be at risk and to replace it with a more authoritarian and directive type of practice. Jordan[9] puts forward a similar analysis of what has taken place in the field of child abuse. However, he stresses that one of the ways in which social workers have coped with this transition has been to treat clients in a more paternalistic and infantilizing fashion. He advocates a more egalitarian approach emphasizing the need for social workers to pay due respect to clients' rights of citizenship and self-determination.

On the other hand, the NSPCC[10] in particular have argued that help to such families cannot be provided without a framework of control and one of the direct consequences of this viewpoint is a preference in nearly all cases for the use of statutory orders. This is in line with the views of those to whom we have previously referred who do not see care and control as incompatible. Such a consensus view is predominant among those writing about child abuse work, though there has been some discussion and doubt as to whether in practice it is feasible for the same person to detect and investigate abuse and to provide therapy for the parents.[11] Certainly there is much current controversy about these issues following the publication of the Jasmine Beckford report. This report is unequivocal with regard to the duties of social workers where the social worker is *in loco parentis* by virtue of a care order and children have been returned to the physical care of their natural parents. In such instances there should be no doubt about the social work role, it is argued. The local authority is still the legal parent. In practice things are not as clear-cut and issues become far more complicated in the vast majority of suspected abuse cases where statutory orders are not in effect.

Criticisms of the Child Abuse System

Just as the issues about social work practice in the field of child abuse have raised controversies, so has the practical working of the system set up to deal with the problem. As has been seen, Parton and Thomas see it as a means of forcing social workers to take a tougher line with families. Individual aspects of the system have received various responses. Central abuse registers have been seen by the DHSS and most agencies as an integral part of the child abuse system and as a fully justified means of providing protection for children as long as certain guidelines and principles are adhered to.[12] However, Geach[13] from a civil liberties standpoint, considers registers to be illiberal and, incidentally, of little effect. Child abuse case conferences have been criticized for not admitting parents or allowing them to put forward their views.[14] Recent research[15] has found that the use of place-of-safety orders has increased suggesting again that social work practice is becoming increasingly authoritarian. Yet the findings of Dingwall *et al.*'s study[16] contradict this notion. Their analysis of children in care figures[17] demonstrates that there has been no proportional increase in committals to care over the past ten years. Their observation of the child abuse system at work points to considerable efforts being made by all health and welfare practitioners to interpret events in ways which are most favourable to parents. This does not mean that they do not treat parents in a paternalistic way, though their study did not consider that issue directly. However, it does point to the content, if not the form, of child abuse work as being less authoritarian than some of its critics have claimed. These, therefore, are some of the issues which form the focus of this study.

Aims of the Study

Five general areas of concern are considered. The first is the extent to which the child abuse system contrains social workers, as argued by Parton and Thomas. It is important to find out whether social workers do find the child abuse system difficult to operate under and if so, why and in what circumstances. It is also important to know what sort of strategies they adopt, if any, in order to cope with and influence the working of the system, and how this affects the functioning of the system as a whole. If indeed the system does constrain social workers and is perceived by them as a cumbersome and unnecessary response in many cases then this may have important policy implications.

A second area of concern is the decision-making process which takes place in case conferences. We have very little empirical knowledge of the range of factors taken into consideration in deciding whether abuse has take place or not. Similarly we know very little about how risk is assessed, about who is influential in decision-making, and about what consistency there is between decisions.

Thirdly it is important to know how social workers put decisions reached in case conferences into action. We know very little about this crucial transition between decision-making and actual practice. For instance, how open and honest are social workers in communicating decisions to families? What sort of difficulties are experienced at this point of interaction? How do social workers negotiate an understandable role with clients? How do they plan their interventions and how successful are they in implementing them?

A fourth area of interest is the progress of cases over a period of time. We know very little about the effectiveness of ongoing intervention into cases of child abuse except for the cases which result in public inquiries. There is a pressing need to estimate to what extent and in what circumstances social workers are successful in practice. For instance, how accurate are the predictions of case conferences and how does the nature of intervention change over time?

Finally the views of the parents who are the subject of child abuse intervention are of importance. To a large extent with the focus on child protection these have been overlooked. While there can be no doubt that child protection must remain the overriding concern the views of parents may prove instructive. For instance, how do they view their experiences with social workers? Do they indeed see them as patronizing and authoritarian as Jordan and Parton respectively have suggested? Or do they see them as helpful people just doing their jobs? Are there qualities that clients prefer in social workers? How easy are relationships?

North City – some socio-economic details

The study took place between 1981 and 1985 mainly in one large metropolitan borough social services department, (North City

Social Services Department). A brief period of study took place in a smaller neighbouring metropolitan borough for comparative purposes, (Smallborough Social Services Department).

North City is an area that has experienced considerable deprivation and decay from Victorian times onwards. These difficulties have been exacerbated in the recession of the last ten to fifteen years. Its geographical location has accelerated the decline and much of its trade and industry has gone to the more affluent south-east following entry into the E.E.C. This relative deprivation is reflected in the unemployment rate which in 1982 was 16.8 per cent compared with a national average of 13.1 per cent. In certain areas of the city the rate of unemployment was, and still is, far higher. A large proportion of the population in the city is housed in council property, a good deal of which is in a considerable state of disrepair.

Twenty two per cent of North City's population consists of children under the age of 15, which is similar to the proportion in the country as a whole. North City had 1811 children in care in 1981, a rate of 13.7 per 1000 children under the age of 18. This compared with a national average of 7.6 per 1000, but was slightly lower than that of other large northern conurbations. These figures do not differentiate between young offenders and children who have been ill-treated and so render generalizations problematic. However, there is some suggestion that even though North City was likely to have a high 'children at risk' population it was relatively restrained in its use of care facilities.

Provision for children

With regard to resources for children in North City, there were two children's hospitals within the city boundaries, one a regional resource, the other a city resource. The latter, situated in an inner-city area, was used almost as a health clinic by the local population, and direct self-referral with minor ailments was the norm.

Day nursery provision in North City was relatively generous compared with the country as a whole and with comparable northern cities. Child abuse cases received priority consideration and some of the nurseries were monitoring large numbers of them.

Voluntary agencies abounded in the city – there were three family centres providing facilities for parents and children in informal settings. Some of the voluntary agencies offered casework and family therapy services. However, it was rare for any of these agencies to be involved with families specifically on account of child abuse. The exceptions to this rule were the Family Service Unit and the

N.S.P.C.C. The latter agency played only a minor part in direct child abuse work in North City. It had only a small number of officers covering a wide region which included North City as one section.

North City Social Services Department and Child Abuse

North City Social Services Department took responsibility for between 90 and 95 per cent of officially recognized child abuse cases.- North City's organizational structure was a functional one.[18] The headquarters were based in the city centre and housed the upper tiers of managerial, administrative and specialist professional staff. Front-line social work practitioners, senior and area officers were situated in 9 community-based district offices. Each area also housed occupational therapists, fostering officers and family aides. In most areas social worker teams were divided into geographically-based long-term teams and intake teams, all operating on a generic basis. In one area division of labour was based on specialist lines. Family and children cases dominated caseloads, a feature common to many generically organized departments.[19] Teams consisted of between 4 and 6 social workers headed by senior social workers with area officers completing the line hierarchy. In addition, specialist consultants, including those in child care, were available on a part-time basis to each district. Overall North City employed 390 social workers.[20] According to the Barclay Report[21], about 70 per cent of front- line workers in England and Wales were qualified in 1980. This was approximately the case in North City. About half of North City's children in care were boarded out, a figure which was higher than for most comparable cities.[22] Residential care was rarely used for younger ill-treated children, a practice which the Beckford Report[23] found in Brent and commented on critically. There was a residential assessment facility available for children aged under 14. North City Social Services Department responded to the D.H.S.S. circulars of 1974 by setting up an Area Review Committee which in turn established a child abuse system consisting of a procedures manual, a central abuse register and a case conference procedure. By 1981 at the start of the study, two principal social workers had responsibility for the management and oversight of the system – a form of organization currently being advocated for general implementation by B.A.S.W.[24] The principal social workers operated from the City Centre Headquarters of the Social Services Department. They administered the central abuse register and kept child abuse records for every case processed through the system. They also, with the aid of a small secretariat, arranged, chaired and minuted case conferences, acted as specialist consultants on child abuse matters and were involved in training and policy issues via representation on the Area Review Committee. They were directly responsible to the assistant director for fieldwork services.

This child abuse section gradually took over more and more of the functions of the child care section which had been in existence since reorganization in 1971. The latter consisted of a principal social worker and three child care consultants, already referred to. By the time of the study a rough division of labour had been established whereby all physical, sexual and emotional abuse cases (including failure to thrive) were dealt with by the child abuse section, whereas neglect cases and other child care matters were dealt with by the child care section. In practice the child abuse section became involved in many of the neglect cases as often several forms of abuse were suspected in one case. Generally many child care cases were being redefined as ones of child abuse. (see Figure 2.1 for an organizational map).

Thus in North City there was a centralized system for dealing with child abuse managed by the statutory social services department. Nationally there are different forms of organization. The N.S.P.C.C. special units provide a co-ordinating and case management service to 10 per cent of the child population.[25] In some areas the responsibility for child abuse management is decentralized with each social services area office administering its child abuse procedures and non-specialist middle managers chairing conferences. In others, though probably a small number, medical personnel chair conferences.[26]

North City deals with approximately 150 'new' cases of child abuse/neglect a year. The vast majority are ones of physical abuse and 75 per cent of the case conferences take place in one or other of the two children's hospitals. The formal aim of North City's system, as for systems nationwide, is one of providing a fail-safe screening of all potential child abuse cases. The official philosophy is heavily weighted towards child protection and the need for all professionals to be vigilant in seeking out child abuse. For instance, North City's procedure manual features on its cover the silhouetted figures of a cowering little girl and a man wielding a belt over her.[27] Most offices had a memorandum on the wall warning social workers that they would be subject to disciplinary procedures if they did not adhere to the instructions outlined in the manual. North City had in the recent past been involved in a public inquiry following the death of a child. However, the atmosphere with regard to procedure following was probably even tighter in Smallborough social

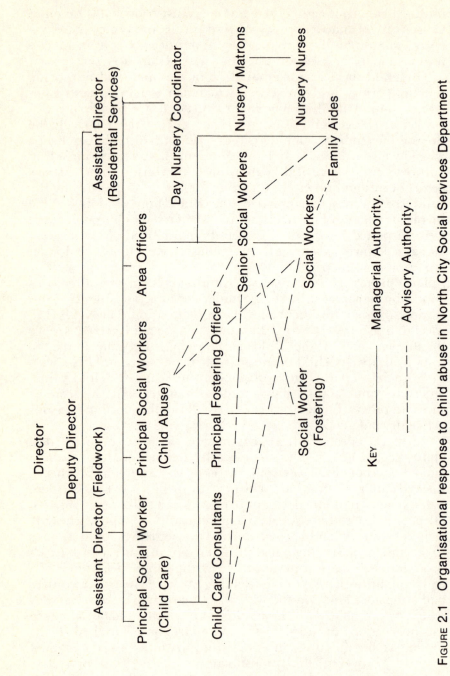

FIGURE 2.1 Organisational response to child abuse in North City Social Services Department

services department which had not gone through a similar experience suggesting that North City's response to child abuse was not atypically rigorous.

Methodology

A pilot study was conducted with eight social work teams from two of the area offices, 6 long-term and two intake teams . Discussions also took place with the principal social workers responsible for child abuse administration and management. Group discussions were held with the teams and their team leaders lasting approximately an hour each. These were tape-recorded and later analysed. The focus of the discussions was the social workers' perceptions of the child abuse system. The findings from these discussions provided a focus for research in the main body of the study. In addition they provided some data on the informal aspects of the child abuse system.

Fifty five case conferences were attended and observed. These were all 'new' conferences, resulting from recent incidents of abuse or neglect. Data was collected from all these conferences drawn from notes taken while the conferences were being conducted.

Twenty five cases were selected from these 55 conferences for follow-up. Initially the aim had been to follow up only those cases in which registration or care proceedings were the outcome. However, such outcomes were relatively rare being decided upon in only a quarter of all case conferences. In addition it became apparent that the dividing line between registered and non-registered cases allocated for social work support was not a very clear one. In consequence the range of cases for study was widened somewhat.

Social workers dealing with these 25 cases were interviewed approximately six weeks after the case conferences. These interviews were tape recorded and later analysed. There were no refusals to co-operate with the study.

Further interviews with social workers took place between six and eight months after the case conferences. In some instances cases had been transferred to new social workers. Again interviews were tape recorded and later analysed. There were no refusals to co-operate.

The child abuse records of these 25 cases were analysed at approximately 2 years after the initial case conferences to check on further officially investigated incidents of abuse.

In addition 99 randomly selected child abuse case records from 1983 were analysed to provide further data and a means of checking the representativeness of the case-study sample with regard to a wider range of officially investigated cases.

Ten of the 25 families who were the subject of the study were interviewed between 9 and 18 months after the initial case conferences. An attempt was made to follow up nearly all families. However, this proved very difficult in many cases because either the social worker or the clients themselves felt it inappropriate. In three of the cases of a highly sensitive nature the presence of a research worker would have been a gross intrusion on people's privacy. Interviews in all but one of the 10 cases were tape-recorded and later analysed.

A period of two weeks was spent in Smallborough, analysing child abuse case notes, interviewing social workers and social work managers, going on visits to families with social workers and attending case conferences. The aim of this largely observational research was to 'see' another system at work, to check if there were major differences in approach and, if so, why.

The data collected by these means will be explored critically in the following chapters.

Notes

1. R. Dingwall *et al.*, (1983), op. cit. – page 213 and note 3.

   Our preference for this term reflects a view that social control has probably become irredeemably contaminated by its recently-acquired pejorative connotations. What we are discussing is the minimal level of self-containment which is essential for the formation of human collectivities.

2. See E. Younghusband, (1978), *Social Work in Britain 1950–75,* Allen & Unwin, Chapter 1 and also J. Packman, (1981), *The Child's Generation,* Blackwell.

3. There has been considerable space devoted to this subject in social work literature. For a compendium of such writing see F.E. McDermott (ed.), 1975, *Self-Determination in Social Work,* Routledge & Kegan Paul. See also R. Plant, (1970), *Social and Moral Theory in Casework,* Routledge & Kegan Paul in which the view is put forward that self-determination in psychoanalytical terms can be seen as a technique of change as well as a human right.

4. F. P. Biestek, (1957), *The Casework Relationship,* Allen & Unwin.

5. See A. Foren & R. Bailey, (1968), *Authority in Social Casework,* Pergamon Press. A more up-to-date discussion of these issues is to be found in P. Day, (1981), *Social Work and Social Control,* Tavistock. See also C.C. Cowger and C.R. Atherton, (1974), 'Social Control. A Rationale for Social Welfare,' *Social Work* 19, 456–62.

6. P. Raynor, (1978), 'Compulsory Persuasion. A Problem for Correctional Social

Work'. *B.J.S.W.* vol. 8 pp. 411–424.

7. See M. Simpkin, (1979), *Trapped Within Welfare*, Macmillan. Ch. 2.

8. N. Parton and T. Thomas, (1983), 'Child Abuse and Citizenship' in B. Jordan and N. Parton (eds), *The Political Dimensions of Social Work*, Blackwell.

9. W. Jordan, (1978), *Freedom and the Welfare State*, Routledge and Kegan Paul.

10. See J. Pickett, (1976), 'The management of non-accidental injury to children in the city of Manchester' in M. Borland (ed.), *Violence in the Family*, Manchester University Press.

11. K. Drews, (1980), 'The Role Conflict of the Child Protective Service Worker: Investigator and Helper', *Child Abuse and Neglect*, vol. 4, no. 4.

12. D.H.S.S., (1980), Child Abuse and Central Register Systems (LASSL (80) 4).

13. H. Geach, (1983), 'Child Abuse Registers: Time for a Change?' in H. Geach and E. Szwed (eds), *Providing Civil Justice for Children*, E. Arnold.

14. This issue is discussed in T. Brown & J. Waters (eds.), (1985) *Parental Participation in Case Conferences.* The British Association for the Prevention and Study of Child Abuse and Neglect.

15. D.H.S.S., (1985), Social Work Decisions in Child Care. Recent Research Findings and Their Implications. H.M.S.O.

16. R. Dingwall, J. Eekelaar and T. Murray, (1983), *The Protection of Children*, Blackwell.

17. R. Dingwall and J. Eekelaar, (1984), 'Rethinking Child Protection' in M.D.A. Freeman (ed.), *State, Law and the Family*, Tavistock.

18. See R. Rowbottom *et al.*, (1974), *Social Services Departments*, Heinemann pp. 68–78. They found two main forms of organizational structure used by social services departments. The 'functional' approach was common to most metropolitan boroughs. Its distinctive features are that lines of authority are based around particular functions of the department and that management is fairly centralized.

19. See D. Howe, (1980), 'Divisions of Labour in Area Teams of Social Services Departments'. *Social Policy and Administration*, vol. 14, no. 2, pp. 133–150.

20. Figures taken from Personal Social Services Statistics 1982–3. Actuals. The Chartered Institute of Public Finance and Accountancy. North City's staff numbers are similar to those of other large northern cities.

21. N.I.S.W., (1982), *Social Workers: Their Roles and Tasks*, Bedford Square Press.

22. See note (20) for source.

23. 'A Child in Trust', The Report of the Panel of Inquiry into the Circumstances surrounding the Death of Jasmine Beckford, (1985), London Borough of Brent.

24. BASW, (1985), *The Management of Child Abuse*, BASW.

25. S. Creighton, (1984), *Trends in Child Abuse.* N.S.P.C.C.

26. See O. Stevenson and C. Hallett, (1980), *Child Abuse: Aspects of Interprofessional Co-ordination*, Allen & Unwin.

27. The pros and cons of such an emotive cover were considered at a meeting of the Area Review Committee which I attended. The prevailing view was that though all abuse was not of the sadistic kind depicted on the manual's cover something dramatic was needed to remind workers of the potential seriousness of all forms of child abuse in order to maintain a high level of vigilance.

Chapter 3

The Parents, their Children and the Social Workers

There are two common misconceptions. One is that we are all potential batterers and that the main causes are depression and poverty. In fact, most parents who violently assault their children are young, immature, ill-educated, disorganised and aggressive; many of the fathers involved have criminal records. (Mia Kellmer-Pringle, (1980), Towards the Prediction of Child Abuse in N. Frude (ed.) *Psychological Approaches to Child Abuse.* (pp. 203/4)

It is strongly argued by some authors that we all carry within us the potential for abuse and that it only requires a sufficient number of stress circumstances or poor controls to spark off similar violent responses. (Letitia Allan, (1978), 'Child Abuse: A critical review of the Research and Theory' in J.P. Martin (ed.) *Violence and the Family* p. 51)

Research into abusing parents and abused children

There has been a wealth of research into the psychological and social characteristics of abusing parents and abused children in an attempt to create a typology that will aid prediction and prevention. Many of the research findings have been controversial and some have been contradictory of each other.[1] For instance, Smith *et al.*[2] found that low parental IQ was associated with child abuse whereas Steele and Pollock[3] found no connnection. Gil[4] found that those from the lower socio-economic classes were disproportionately represented among officially recognized child abusers, yet those in Steele and

Pollock's and Lynch and Roberts'[5] samples came from a wide spread of social backgrounds. As Allan[6] has pointed out, 'research into child abuse is almost continually haunted by the possibility of sample bias'. Some samples are drawn from cases of serious abuse only as, for example, in Baldwin and Oliver's study.[7] Others such as that of Gil, referred to above, include a wide range of cases of both moderate and serious abuse. It is extremely problematic to make general statements about 'abusive families' from such studies.

Nevertheless, and bearing these methodological difficulties in mind, several research studies do consistently point towards certain factors being associated with child abuse. Marital problems,[8] the young age of mothers at birth,[9] neo-natal problems,[10] social isolation,[11] deprivation of parents as children[12] and children who do not respond well to parents at an early age[13] have all been indicated. Again it must be stressed that while such factors may be helpful in alerting professionals to potentially worrying situations, great care should be taken in using them as predictors. Parton[24] is particularly critical of the claims made by Kempe based on his study of 350 children born at Colorado General Hospital.[15] He points out that the assertion of a 79 per cent success prediction rate of parents likely to abuse their children hides the fact that 'for every person correctly identified another one will be mislabelled'. He goes on to point out that the high success rate is rendered even more dubious by the fact that the definition of abuse used is 'enormously broad and all-inclusive', and many of the cases defined as abusive by Kempe would not be so defined by professionals working in this field.

Parents and Children in this Study – some general facts

This study was not specifically designed with a view to examining the characteristics of abusing parents. Nevertheless it is important to give an overall impression of the 25 case-study families in question.

It should be stated clearly that the parents in this study were very much 'a mixed bag' in the sense that, after investigation, four were not thought to have abused their children, but still to be in need of social work intervention. A further 16 were considered to have abused their children, but there was no equivocal evidence that they had done so and no admission, and only in two cases was abuse actually admitted (see Table 3.1). As referred to before, the fact that the majority of parents denied that they had abused their children made social work practice difficult and placed it on a very uncertain

Table 3.1   Grounds for intervention

	No.	Per cent
1. Abuse denied, account accepted, social worker to visit	4	16
2. Abuse denied, account not accepted, social worker to visit.	2	8
3. Abuse denied, account not accepted, social worker to visit, register.	9	36
4. Abuse denied, account not accepted, care proceedings	5	20
5. Abuse admitted, register	1	4
6. Abuse admitted, care proceedings	1	4
	22	88

standing. This was still true even if a statutory order was in force following care proceedings – particularly with regard to specific therapeutic help. If a parent continued to deny abuse, it was impossible to tackle problems directly.

Of the three remaining cases, one was a conference on an unborn child and the other two were concerned with allegations of sexual abuse against foster-parents who denied the accusations.

Table 3.2, 3.3 and 3.4 show the representativeness of the study sample compared with a sample of 150 cases dealt with by the two child abuse systems that were the subject of this study.[16]

As can be seen from Table 3.2, which gives the reasons for conferences being held, the study sample as a whole is skewed toward the more serious end of the spectrum of abuse.

The study sample includes a higher percentage of cases of serious physical abuse (33 per cent compared with 14 per cent) and fewer cases of moderate abuse (33 per cent compared with 53 per cent). Such a view is confirmed by an examination of the outcomes of conferences (see Table 3.3). Twenty two per cent of the wider sample cases resulted in no further action being taken at all. No cases of this kind were considered for the case-study sample as the intention was to examine cases in which social work involvement was likely to last for at least six months. Furthermore, whereas 43.5 per cent of the wider sample cases were allocated to social workers to be monitored without registration this was true in only 28 per cent of the study

Table 3.2 Reasons for holding case conferences

Reason	Study sample (n=25)		Data from child abuse case records (n=150)	
	No.	Per cent	No.	Per cent
1. Moderate physical injury*	9	33	79	53
2. Severe physical injury*	9	33	21	14
3. Sexual Abuse	3	11	20	13
4. Physical Neglect	3	11	13	9
5. Emotional Abuse	1	4	5	3
6. Sched. 1. Offender	1	4	9	6
7. Other	1	4	3	2
Total	27**	100	150	100

NOTE
*Definitions used by NSPCC.[17]
**In two cases two reasons were given.

Table 3.3 Case conference outcomes

Outcome	Study sample (n=25)		Data from child abuse case records (n=150)	
	No.	Per cent	No.	Per cent
No further action	0	0	32	22
Social worker to monitor	7	28	67	43.5
Register Decision	11	44	32	22
Care proceedings	5	20	18	12
Other	2*	8	1	0.5
Total	25	100	150	100

NOTE
* In one case wardship proceedings were initiated and in the other children were already in care with foster parents at the time of the incident.

Table 3.4   The ages of the children who were subjects of case conferences

Age	Study sample (n=27)		Data from child abuse records (n=182)	
	No.	Per cent	No.	Per cent
Unborn	1	4	5	3
Up to 1 yr	6	22	20	11
1 yr–5 yr	13	48	61	33.5
6 yr–10 yr	5	18.5	43	23.5
11 yr–15 yr	2	7.5	38	21
16 yr–17 yr	0	0	15	8
	27	100	182	100

sample. The rate of registration of cases in the study sample was twice as high as that for the wider sample. It is clear, therefore, that the study sample as a whole, is not typical of general child abuse work carried out in a social services department, but is more representative of the middle to serious range.

Ages of Children

Table 3.4 gives the ages of the children in the study sample who were the subjects of the case conferences and of those from the wider sample. In general, the children in the study sample were younger than those of the wider sample. This was probably a result of the fact that more serious cases were included in this sample. Allan[18] points out that the majority of studies indicate that a child is most vulnerable between the age of 3 months and 3 years. She quotes Gelles[19] as arguing that children of that age are more likely to be frustrating to parents and, therefore, provoke more hostility, whereas Gil[20] accounts for these statistics by suggesting that younger children are more likely to be severely injured when hit.

Family Structure

Table 3.5 gives a breakdown of the family structure of the families in the study sample.

Table 3.5 Parents of children in sample study (n=25)

	No.	Per cent
Child living with father and mother	10	40
Child living with mother and either step-father or cohabitive	4	12
Child living with mother alone	8	32
Child living with mother and other relatives	2	8
Child with father	0	0
Other**	1	4
Total	25	100

NOTE
*Includes unborn baby
**Children living in long term foster home

Only half of the sample lived with a mother and father figure and only 40 per cent with both their natural parents. This figure is far lower than the national average[21] and is perhaps indicative of the fact that many of the parents and children in this sample were experiencing considerable stress and upheaval. A higher percentage of children lived with both their natural parents in the wider sample.

There were 53 children in the 25 families, an average of 2.12 children per family, about the same ratio as in the wider sample but slightly larger than the national average.[22] Table 3.6 gives a breakdown of these figures.

Over 70 per cent of the families had two children or less. It has been suggested that large family size is associated with abuse.[23] However, there is no evidence to support such a view in the figures from either the study or wider sample in this research.

Age of Parents

Parental age has been another factor given considerable attention by child abuse researchers. Baldwin and Oliver[24] in their study of serious abuse cases found that a high proportion of mothers were

Table 3.6   No. of children in each household

No. of children	No. of families	Per cent
0*	1	4
1	8	32
2	9	36
3	5	20
5	1	4
8	1	4
Total	25	100

NOTE
*Unborn child.

very young at the time of marriage or cohabitation. Smith *et al.*[25] found that 54 per cent of mothers in their study had had children before the age of 20. Lynch[26] found the same in 40 per cent of her sample. Table 3.7 provides details of mothers' ages at the birth of their first child. Over half had had children by the age of 20. At the time of the case conferences, however, the average age of the men in the households was 28.6 years and that of the women 26.9 years.

Employment and Housing

Of the men in the household three quarters were unemployed. Of the 25 women, 22 were unemployed as well. Twenty of the 25 families were in receipt of supplementary benefit while only 4 families depended solely on earnings for their livelihood. Those in work were in unskilled occupations. Data concerning occupations from the wider sample was not reliable. With regard to housing, 17 of the families lived in council owned accommodation while only 3 were owner-occupiers. Seventeen of the 25 families were housed in flats or maisonettes, many of which were on the first floor or higher. Housing was mentioned by social workers as a source of stress in 6 of the 25 cases. It is not possible to estimate any more accurately the effect of housing on the families in the study. Most of the clients interviewed in the research lived in structurally sound homes but material standards and the immediate environment were poor in the eyes of a middle-class researcher.

Table 3.7   Age of mothers at birth of first child

Age	Number of Mothers
14	1
17	4
18	5
19	4
20–22	4
23–26	4
27–30	2
Total	22*

NOTE
*In 2 cases it was not clear. The first child had either died or been adopted. One of the 'mothers' was a foster-parent with no natural children.

Support Systems

Some consideration was given to the support systems available to the families in the sample study. As has been mentioned previously, Garbarino[27] has pointed to a connection between isolation and abuse. However, the whole notion of support is a problematic one. Hardly any of the families in the study were completely isolated. Virtually all were born in North City and had not moved far from their families of origin. Most of them had contact with their extended families. In 16 of the 25 cases, extended families were geographically very close – in several cases in the same street or only a few streets away. Judging whether this proximity and 'contact' led to supportive relationships or not was difficult – information was derived from social work accounts rather than direct questioning of clients. The social workers tended to view contacts as unsupportive if there was conflict or if it was felt that the client's ability to cope was being undermined by an unhelpful parent. Such judgements tended to dismiss the value of at least some contact with the extended family which except in the most extreme cases was often better than no contact at all. Accepting, therefore, that such judgements probably underestimated the degree of support derived from extended families, it was found that in just over half the cases support was forthcoming from at least one of the families. In 5 of the 25 cases contact with extended families was 'neutral' or 'luke-warm' and in 5 it was considered to be hostile. The lone parents were no more isolated in this sense than were the 2-parent families.

Support from neighbours (or lack of it) can also be seen as making some contribution to the stress experienced by a family. In three of the 25 cases, neighbours actually reported the incident of alleged abuse or neglect to the authorities. (In two of these cases relationships with them had previously been harmonious). Overall, 5 of the families in the study had hostile relationships with their neighbours and 2 had no contact at all. Seven were considered to have good relationships with their neighbours. It was very difficult to develop a clear picture on this issue. Some parents gained an adverse reputation if it became known that they had neglected or abused their children and this placed extra pressure on them and in a few instances resulted in their moving to a different street or district. Nevertheless, most of the families in this study had relatively normal contacts with those in their locality. They were not geographically isolated and they did not, for the most part, stand out in the community as being overtly poorer than the rest of the population.

Families' Previous Contact with Social Services Departments

Twenty two of the families had had contact with social services departments prior to the incident of suspected abuse that led to the case conference being held as can be seen from Table 3.8. Of these, 18 had had involvement with social services department as a result of concern over child care problems defined as child abuse, and ten were ongoing cases where there was current concern. Eight of these cases had already been the subjects of child abuse case conferences (2 on two occasions). The details are listed in Table 3.9.

The sample study, therefore, consists of a population, most of which had had some contact with social services departments prior to the current incident (88 per cent). Just over half had had considerable previous contact as a result of suspected child abuse. Indeed, those who had had previous and current ongoing contact over child abuse (13 in all) had on average been visited by social workers for just over three years. It is fairly clear, therefore, that for some of the clients in this study, the initial case conference which formed the starting point of this research was their first contact with the child abuse system whereas others already had considerable experience either of social work intervention over child care matters

Table 3.8   Families previous contact with social services departments

Reason	No.	Per cent
1. No contact	3	12
2. Previous referrals (not child abuse)	1	4
3. Previous ongoing contact (not child abuse)	1	4
4. Current ongoing contact (not child abuse)	2	8
5. Previous referral (child abuse)	5	20
6. Previous ongoing contact (child abuse)	3	12
7. Current ongoing contact (child abuse)	10	40
Total	25	100

Table 3.9   Previous child abuse case conferences held on study sample

Time prior to current conference	Case No.	Reason for holding	Outcome
6 yrs	23	Physical Abuse	Care Proceedings
5 yrs	10	Infanticide	Prosecution Register
3 yrs	12	Physical abuse by cohabitee	Register, Social Worker to monitor
2 yrs	23	Conference on Newborn Child	Register, Social Worker to monitor
2 yrs	11	Neglect	Social Worker to monitor
1 yr	12	Physical abuse by cohabitee	Social Worker to monitor
1 yr	17	Allegation of physical abuse	Social Worker to monitor
6 months	16	Emotional neglect	Register, Social Worker to monitor
3 months	21	Physical abuse allegation	Register, Social Worker to monitor
2 months	3	Physical abuse allegation	Register, Social Worker to monitor

or of the child abuse system (or both) at this stage. Indeed children from six of the families were already registered at this time.

Data regarding previous contacts with social services departments was taken from the wider sample of 150 cases in North City and Smallborough. The figures in Table 3.10 show that a higher percentage of the families in the sample study had previous child abuse history than was true of the wider sample. It is also interesting to note from Table 3.10 that North City's cases as a whole have more past history of abuse or suspected abuse than those in Smallborough.

Table 3.10 Families' previous contact with social services departments
North City (n=99), Smallborough SSDS (n=51)

Type of contact	North City No.	North City Per cent	Smallborough No.	Smallborough Per cent	Total No.	Total Per cent
1. Not known previously	36	36.4	21	42	57	38
2. Previous work with family (general)	17	17.2	16	32	33	22
3. Previous work with family (Child Abuse)	46	46.4	14	28	60	40
Total	99	100	51	100	150	100

Parents in Care

Finally, mention should be made of the fact that 5 of the fathers in the study (nearly 50 per cent) and 5 of the mothers (20 per cent) had themselves experienced periods in residential care as children. In 4 families, both parents had been in care. In the main, the men had been in care as a result of criminal offending, the women because of family breakdown or neglect. Using data from the wider sample in North City, 16 of the 99 mothers had been in care as children and 4 of the men. (These figures are likely to underestimate the true figure as such factors were not consistently recorded in the case files). Both samples clearly contain more deprived parents (assuming care to be an indicator of deprivation) than the population at large.

The Social Workers – ages and qualifications

Twenty six social workers dealt with the 25 sample study cases during the period of the study. Twenty of the 26 workers were female and the average age of all workers was 33.30 years. Nineteen of the 26 were qualified. Table 3.11 gives a breakdown of their working grades.

Teams and case-loads

Most teams in North City were either long-term care teams or intake teams. Teams were organized on specialist lines in only one of the nine districts. In principle the long-term care teams dealt with the whole range of client groups. In practice case-loads were dominated by children and families cases. Table 3.12 enumerates the type of teams in which the social workers were situated.

On average there were 4.3 officially recognized child abuse cases per caseload. On average intake team workers estimated that 20 per cent of their time was spent on child abuse work while 48 % was the figure suggested by social workers in long term teams. Two of the workers, one from the NSPCC, specialized in child abuse work. For the rest, child abuse work, while not a specialism, was considered high priority work by the agency and so took up a large part of their time.

Table 3.11   Work grades of social workers in sample study

Volunary agency Social Worker	2	8
Social Worker level 1*	1	4
2*	11	46
3*	10	42
Senior Social Worker	1	4
Principal Social Worker	1	4
Total	24	100

NOTE
*For a description of these job levels see note [28]. The 19 qualified social workers had on average 4.2 years post qualification experience, and 3.6 years pre-qualification experience. The 7 non-qualified social workers had a total of 47 years social work experience (including residential work).

Working with Child Abuse

Table 3.12 Teams in which social workers were situated

Type of team	No.	Per cent
Intake	6	24
S.S.D. Long term	14	64
Other	1	4
Hospital	2	8
Voluntary agency	2	8
Total	25	100

Training

With regard to training the social services department organized a one-week training course on child abuse for all social work staff which they were expected to attend triennially. Virtually all the social workers in the study had attended one of these and most remembered that the courses had focused on recognizing signs of non-accidental injury and carrying out investigations according to the procedures manual. With only one or two exceptions the qualified social workers in the sample study were critical of the small amount of time devoted to child abuse work on their initial social work training courses. Over all 10 of the 24 social workers felt adequately trained including 2 of the unqualified workers. Of those who did feel adequately trained the majority felt that this was a result of working experience rather than of formal training.

The main source of support and advice to social workers was without doubt their seniors or team leaders. The principal social workers for child abuse were also contacted fairly often but largely for procedural advice. General child care consultants were not greatly used for advice or support in this field of work. Other social work colleagues were also seen to be a source of help.

Summary and Conclusion

Parents and Children

Most of the facts and figures point to the study sample being representative overall of the middle to serious end of child abuse work. In the past, information from cases of severe abuse has been used to shape and influence the response to all child abuse situations and much of our knowledge regarding 'abusive parents' derives from studies of cases of serious abuse. The sample in this study reflects a broader spectrum than that. However, judged in comparison with the wider samples of cases dealt with by the system this sample is still skewed towards the serious end of the spectrum.

Bearing this in mind the main features of the study sample were as follows –

1. Most of the parents denied abusing their children and the evidence was rarely unequivocal.
2. In approximately two-fifths of the cases severe physical injuries or neglect were the reason for investigation.
3. Over two-thirds of the sample were responded to by either registration or statutory proceedings.
4. Three-quarters of the children who were the subjects of investigation were aged 5 and under.
5. A higher than normal proportion of families were either lone parent families or reconstituted nuclear families.
6. The families had above average numbers of children, but overall the average was still only 2.12.
7. Over half of the mothers had had children before the age of 20 which is a higher proportion than the national average.
8. Extended families and support from neighbours were present in many cases though this was a complex variable to measure.
9. Most of the families (more than in the wider sample) had had previous contact of different kinds with social services departments and 2/5ths of them were being visited because of suspicion of child abuse at the time of the new incident.
10. Over 1/5th of the parents in the study had themselves had some experience of residential care as children.

Social Workers

The social workers in this sample study were overall female (77 per cent) and qualified (73 per cent) with between 6 and 7 years experience. They had developed skills in child abuse work from practical experience rather than from theoretical training and most spent nearly half of their time working with various types of child abuse work, receiving most of their support and help from fellow social workers and their senior officers.

Notes

1. See L.J. Allan, (1978), 'Child Abuse: A critical review of the Research and the Theory' in J.P. Martin (ed.), *Violence and the Family*, J. Wiley. See also N. Parton, (1985), *The Politics of Child Abuse* ch. 6, B. Blackwell.
2. S.M. Smith, R. Hanson and S. Noble, (1974), 'Social Aspects of the Battered Baby Syndrome', *British Journal of Psychiatry* Vol. 125, pp. 568-82.
3. B.F. Steele and C.B. Pollock, (1968), 'A Psychiatric Study of Parents who Abuse Infants and Small Children', in R.E. Helfer and C.H. Kempe (eds), *The Battered Child*, University of Chicago.
4. D. Gil, (1970), *Violence Against Children*, Harvard University Press.
5. M.A. Lynch and J. Roberts, (1982), *The Consequences of Child Abuse*, Academic Press.
6. L.J. Allan, (1978), op. cit.
7. J.A. Baldwin and J.E. Oliver, (1975), 'Epidemology and family characteristics of severely abused children', *British Journal of Preventive and Social Medicine*, 29 pp. 205-221.
8. See N. Lukianowicz, (1971), 'Battered Children', *Psychiatria Clinica*, 4, 257-280.
9. See S.M. Smith *et al.*, (1974), op. cit. also J.A. Baldwin and J.E. Oliver, (1975), op. cit.
10. See E. Elmer, (1967), *Children in Jeopardy*, University of Pittsburg Press and M. Lynch, J. Roberts and M. Gordon (1976) 'Early warning of Child Abuse', *Dev. Medicine and Child Neurology*, December.
11. See J. Garbarino and C. Gilliam, *Understanding Abusive Families*, (Lexington Books, 1980) – also A.E. Skinner and R.L. Castle, (1969), 'Seventy Eight Battered Children: A Retrospective Study', London NSPCC.
12. See Steele and Pollock, (1968), op. cit. and E. Baher *et al.*, (1976), *At Risk: An Account of the Work of the Battered Child Research Department*, London, Routledge and Kegan Paul.
13. See C. Ounsted, R. Oppenheimer and J. Lindsay, (1975), 'The Psychopathology and psychotherapy of the familes: Aspects of bonding families', in A.W. Franklin (ed), *Concerning Child Abuse*, Churchill Livingstone.
14. N. Parton, (1985), op. cit. pp. 141-143.
15. R.S. and C.H. Kempe, (1978), *Child Abuse*, Fontana/Open Books ch. 5.
16. Data for the wider sample was taken from case records in North City social services department in 1983 and Smallborough Social Services department in 1984. In 1983, over 150 'new' incidents of child abuse were the subjects of case conferences in North City – 99 of these were selected at random for study. In 1984 Smallborough SSD held 51 'new incident' child abuse case conferences. All these were analysed making a total of 150 cases in all.

17. See S.J. Creighton, (1984), *Trends in Child Abuse*, NSPCC. According to Creighton, "Serious abuse is defined as: all fractures, head injuries, internal injuries, severe burns and ingestion of toxic substances. Moderate abuse is defined as: all soft tissue injuries of a superficial nature."
18. L.J. Allan, (1978), op. cit.
19. R.J. Gelles, (1973), 'Child Abuse as Psychopathology: a sociological critique and reformulation', *American Journal of Orthopsychiatry*, 43, 611-21.
20. D.J. Gil, (1970), op. cit.
21. In 1983 it was estimated that 5 per cent of all families were lone parents with dependent children, whereas married couples with dependent children formed 30 per cent of all families. *Social Trends* (1985) HMSO No. 15.
22. In 1983 there was an average of 1.9 dependent children per married couple family. *Social Trends* (1985) HMSO No. 15.
23. NSPCC, (1976), Registers of Suspected Non-Accidental Injury. Battered Child Research Dept. RKP.
24. J.A. Baldwin and J.E. Oliver, (1975), op. cit.
25. S.M. Smith *et al.*, (1974), op. cit.
26. M. Lynch, (1975), 'Ill Health and Child Abuse', *The Lancet* 16 Aug. 317.
27. J.M. Garbarino and G. Gilliam, (1980), op. cit.
28. *Level 1 Social Workers* are those who under close and regular supervision are expected to manage a caseload: which may include all client groups and all but the more vulnerable individuals or those with complex problems; assess, plan and implement action or treatment. Such social workers are not expected to make decisions affecting the liberty of clients or in relation to place of safety orders.

    Level 2 Social Workers are those who with supervision and advice are expected to manage a caseload which may include the more vulnerable clients or those with complex problems and may be expected to accept responsibility for action in relation to the liberty or safety of clients in emergency.

    Level 3 Social Workers are those who with access to advice and within normal arrangements for professional accountability are expected to take full responsibility for managing a caseload which will include the more vulnerable clients or those with particularly complex problems in situations where personal liberty or safety is at stake. Such officers are expected to concentrate on specific areas of work requiring more developed skills. These levels were used as the basis of agreement between unions and employers during the social work strike of 1978/79 and are still in operation.

    See The Proposals p. 3. *Social Work Today* vol. 10, No. 23, 6.2.79.

Chapter 4

Detecting and Investigating Child Abuse

On the one hand is the compassionate approach to abuse. Human service professionals who treat violence and abuse from this perspective approach it with an abundance of human kindness and a nonpunitive outlook on intervention. The compassionate philosophy views the parents as victims themselves. The cause of the abuse may be seen in social and developmental origins, and not in the abuser. Abusive parents, rather than being seen as cold, cruel monsters, are seen as sad, deprived, needy human beings. Compassionate intervention involves supporting the abuser and his or her family. Home-maker services, health and child care, and other supports are made available to the family.

On the other hand is the control model. The control model involves aggressive use of intervention to limit, and, if necessary, punish the deviant violent behaviour. The control approach places full responsibility for actions with the abuser. Control involves removal of the child from the home, separation of the abused wife from her violent spouse, and full criminal prosecution of the offender. (Richard Gelles and Claire Cornell, (1985), *Intimate Violence in Families,* p. 133.

Introduction

In the U.S.A. reporting laws are the mechanism whereby the State ensures that health, welfare and other public agencies are vigilant about, and respond responsibly to, child abuse. These laws place a mandatory duty on such agencies to report child abuse to the child protection services – failure to do so is a prosecutable offence. In Great Britain no such laws exist. The local Authority has a duty to investigate allegations of child abuse, as laid down in Section 2(1) of the Children and Young Persons Act 1969 – 'If a local Authority receive information suggesting that there are grounds for bringing care proceedings in respect of a child or young person who resides or is found in their area, it shall be the duty of that Authority to cause enquiries to be made into the case unless they are satisfied that such enquiries are unnecessary'. However, there is no mandatory duty placed on agencies such as health authorities, education departments and the police to report cases of child abuse to local authorities. Heavy reliance has been placed on the notion of professional duty and also on the climate of fear surrounding child abuse to ensure that the right response is made. In general there has been satisfaction with this way of operating. Indeed in many of the cases subject to public inquiries concern has focused not on responses to initial reports of abuse, but rather on ongoing work with families where abuse has already taken place.[1]

Nevertheless, there is still some debate as to whether such reporting should be introduced in Great Britain. The report of the Beckford inquiry[2] toys with the notion of recommending the use of such laws and concludes –

> Conceding that statutory obligation might be no more than cosmetic, we do think, however, that the statutory declaration of the duty to inform would give expression to society's deep concern that health professionals should play their part in bringing child abuse cases to the notice of Social Services.

They go on to recommend consultation with the professional bodies concerned.

Child Abuse Procedure Manuals

In the absence of reporting laws, one of the key instruments in ensuring alertness of response to child abuse is that of procedural guidelines which are issued to all health, welfare and police agencies in an area. Reference has already been made to those issued by North City Area Review Committee and the emotive nature of the design on its cover. The tone of this document is one of urgency impressing on the various agencies the seriousness of child abuse, the need for vigilance and strict adherence to the guidelines. As if recognizing the problems this type of work creates for welfare professionals the

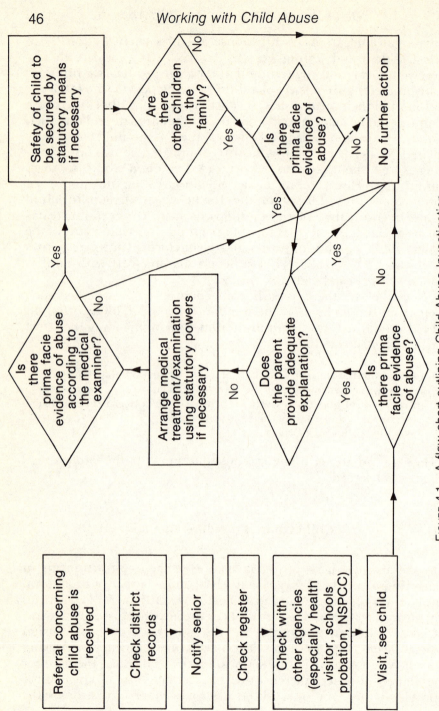

FIGURE 4.1 A flow chart outlining Child Abuse Investigation

manual states – 'A sceptical approach is prudent, although this may be contrary to many professionals' trusting attitudes'.

The flow-chart which is shown in Figure 4.1 outlines the steps required to be taken by North City social services department social workers. The main requirement placed on other agency workers (e.g. Health visitors, general practitioners, probation officers and education personnel) was to involve social services departments as soon as possible.

In theory, therefore, there is a clear-cut guide to investigating allegations of child abuse. As will be seen, however, in practice social workers find it hard to adhere to these procedures which leave many problematic practical and ethical questions unan- swered. In this chapter attention will be focused on the realities of child abuse investigations seen mainly through the eyes of social work practitioners and those of the parents who in fact are the subjects of these investigations.

There is much controversy surrounding this aspect of child abuse work. Social workers have been criticized for being both overzealous and underreactive in investigating abuse. Parton, for instance, argues that 'Social work practice with children and families has become far more authoritative and decisive and has increasingly come to intervene in ways which can be experienced by families as threats or punishments'. He cites the increase in number of place of safety orders as objective evidence to support this view.[3] Yet, Dingwall *et al.*[4] reach a very different conclusion on the basis of their research into the processing of child abuse cases – 'The central fact to be explained by any analysis of decision-making in child protection is the rarity of allegations of mistreatment'. They argue that clinical and social criteria would suggest the existence of many more cases of abuse than actually do get processed through the system. That they do not get processed is attributed to 'a rule of optimism' that staff tend to operate.[5] They go on to contend that two devices facilitate this – the notion of *cultural relativism* which makes it problematic to apply agreed normative standards of assessment and that of *natural love* which is seen as a basic fact of children/parent relationships and as a consequence tends to obscure or devalue evidence to the contrary. These two conflicting views will be considered using data from the 25 cases and discussions with teams of social workers. Two other considerations will be 1) the extent to which the system (and, in particular, the procedural guidelines,) help or hinder social workers in their practice and 2) the views of a small number of clients about being on the 'receiving end'.

How cases get referred

As mentioned earlier, 16 of the 25 families in the case-study had had some previous contact with the social services department because of child care problems. Thirteen of these were 'open' ongoing cases at the time of the new suspected incident of abuse. However, despite this most of the cases were not referred in the first place as a result of agency intervention. Table 4.1 lists the initial referrers.

Table 4.1 Initial references
of abuse incident

Parents	12	(48%)
Victim	1	(4%)
Relatives	1	(4%)
Neighbours	5	(20%)
Nursery	3	(12%)
Police	2	(8%)
School	1	(4%)
	25	

Table 4.2 details the agency first contacted by the initial referrers.

Table 4.2 First referral point for
suspected cases of abuse

Hospital	8	(32%)
Social Services Department	7	(28%)
Health Clinic	4	(12%)
Police	2	(8%)
NSPCC	1	(4%)
FSU	1	(4%)
Health Visitor	1	(4%)
GP	1	(4%)
	25	

Seventy six per cent of the cases were first referred by lay people, not professionals. Home visitors such as social workers, health visitors or others did not initially refer any of the cases in the study.

The parents who referred themselves all went directly to medical services. None referred themselves to the social services department. The latter's referrals all came from other agencies. The 2 referrals to the police came from parents, both cases of suspected sexual abuse, one involving siblings in the family, the other an allegation against a foster-parent. Eventually 17 of the 25 cases received medical examinations. Of the 8 that did not 4 were neglect cases, 3 were sexual abuse cases and one that of an unborn child.

All but 3 cases were eventually referred to the social services department – 2 of these three were followed up by medical social workers and one by a social worker from a voluntary agency.

This stage of intervention could, therefore, be seen as a sorting out process. Referrals came initially mainly from the public – all the cases of physical abuse received hospital examination and all cases ultimately were referred to social services department social workers or others for intervention/assessment prior to case conferences. Less than a third were the subject of police investigation and there were only two prosecutions of parents. It was rare, therefore, for the social workers in the case-study to have to follow the procedures outlined in Figure 4.1 in their entirety. However, it is instructive to look at the guidelines step-by-step to see how they were put into operation.

Checking Records and Registers

Data for this section is derived from the group discussions with social work teams. Checking with district records was seen by social workers as an automatic, non-problematic activity. While, as will be seen later, several social workers demonstrated awareness of the dysfunctional effects of labelling, previous records were still considered important sensitizers to the possibility of abuse. It should be pointed out, however, that in most cases where previous abuse had occurred it was likely that a social worker would be working with the family anyway. The importance of district records became more apparent if the social worker concerned was not available at the time of the referral. Similarly notifying the senior social worker was considered a non-problematic activity – most social workers worked very closely with their immediate supervisors particularly in the early stages of child abuse work both for purposes of support and

accountability. To that extent the guidelines were really unnecessary.

Contacting the central abuse register however, was seen as a more
confused and problematic issue. Firstly, it was not considered
necessary in all cases, because of the practice of maintaining up-to-
date registers at district level. A secondary factor was that, as
perceived by some social workers, checking with the register led to a
check on them and their activities and therefore, they avoided it. One
social worker expressed this view as follows –

> Well you do it (check with the register) and they ring the seniors back.
> That's the register's policy. They won't give you information on the
> phone – they have to ring you back and they always ring the senior.
> And the reason for that – they tell me – is to make sure the senior
> knows what's going on.

Another practice which made the social workers tentative about
consulting the register was that all inquiries to it were logged
leading to subsequent checks from the headquarters office as to what
had happened with regard to particular cases. While some social
workers, mindful of the risk factors involved in child abuse work,
accepted these checks, others resented the need for their professional
activity to be so closely monitored, as they saw it.

Another factor which acted as a deterrent to checking with the
register was that of the amplificatory effect of such an action. This
view is exemplified in the following comments made by a social
worker –

> You have to try and work round it because you're scared of putting
> things into this very heavy machinery. It just takes off really – goes out
> of your control – so you try and avoid it as much as possible.

This worker's fear was partly that of loss of control of decision-
making on his part but also concern that the very fact of putting a
case into the system might result in more serious consequences than
were initially warranted in his opinion.

As a consequence of all these factors, checking with the register on
the part of social workers was a rare event. The B.A.S.W. study of
child abuse registers[6] found similar objects raised by social workers
and other studies have reported very low usage rates of registers.[7]

Checking with other agencies also raised some problems with
some social workers. For instance one social worker argued that he
'wouldn't go to any other agency outside the department until I was
sure there was something wrong'. This was perhaps an extreme view
and much seemed to depend on the quality of trust established

between agencies at local levels. Justification for such an approach lies in a strict interpretation of preserving client confidentiality which makes child abuse investigations highly problematical. Most social workers took a more flexible line.

Confronting Parents

With regard to visiting families and assessing whether abuse had taken place, the procedural guidelines emphasized the need to establish a) prima-facie evidence of abuse and b) the plausibility of the parent's accounts of how the signs of abuse came about. Depending on the social worker's judgement of these two factors (along with information from the checks referred to in the previous section) the child was normally taken to one of the two children's hospitals for medical examination. Most social workers found this investigative role extremely uncomfortable.

> The worst thing that I found is where the child has been injured and the parents are under suspicion and actually confronting parents with the fact and trying to do it in a relatively non-judgemental way and just not trying to be too heavy about the whole thing; I found that difficult.

Most of the social workers interviewed in the study had, however, despite their unease in this role, reconciled themselves to it, so much so that they were critical of other professionals who they felt to be inexperienced in child abuse investigations and therefore, too permissive.

> I remember a terrible occasion when I went in with a health visitor who immediately started back-pedalling and started saying things that you knew you couldn't fulfil like... 'Oh well, we'll just forget about it', which we couldn't. I'd much rather go with one of my colleagues who I knew was going to handle it the same way as I would, rather than with someone who isn't as used to doing it and so is not aware of the procedures and things you have to do.

Nevertheless, there was still a certain amount of ambivalence about the benefits to be gained from close adherence to the procedural guidelines.

Data taken from the group discussions with social workers suggested that, paradoxically, moderate instances of abuse were more likely to be responded to in cases where there was no previous history of abuse than was true of already known cases being visited by social workers. In other words social workers were prepared to take more risks where they felt they knew a family than where they did not. This was done to avoid invoking the full weight of the system and, as the social workers saw it, the possibility of an overreaction. The following account exemplifies some of the thinking behind such a view –

> I've got two where we know in fact that injuries were caused – but they weren't particularly severe injuries even though they were enough for them to be taken off to the doctor, but we still didn't case conference it because of the extraordinary pressures that people were in at the time – the pressures they were under. What we did was change the level of support in those cases – quite considerably, but that wasn't done by any case conference decision.

Other social workers demonstrated an awareness of the risks and problems associated with such an approach –

> There's a danger of a certain amount of collusion when you've known a family for long and not wanting to believe that people you've been working with in a certain way could, or have, perpetrated, particular injuries.

The social worker who made this statement was more prepared than the previous one to allow the system to check on her judgement and more willing to share the case with other people.

Despite these comments made by social workers in the team discussions, in practice in only 3 of the 25 cases considered in detail was there doubt or disagreement on the social worker's part that the child abuse procedures should have been invoked. Two of these were cases of moderate suspicious physical injuries, both bruising to the face, and 1 a case of children potentially being at physical and emotional risk. In two of these cases the social workers felt that health visitors were overreacting to a situation and in the other, a case being supervised by a voluntary agency worker, who ultimately did invoke the system, there was concern as to whether such a formal response would worsen relations between her and her clients thereby increasing the risks to the child.

One of these cases raised many of the issues just referred to. It concerned a lone parent, aged 19, living with 2 children, aged 18 months and 6 months. She had been receiving social work help for several months after a suicide attempt. She had been helped with rehousing, sorting out finances and general emotional support. She took her child to the nursery with a large red mark on the side of his face. The child was referred to the hospital where a paediatrician assessed the injury as being non-accidental. As a result, the child was detained in hospital and a case conference called. The senior social worker in the case strongly disagreed with the need to call a case conference. To her, it was evident that this was purely and simply a case of overchastisement by a woman who had poor parenting skills and was experiencing considerable environmental stress. As social workers were already involved and in constant touch with the situation she saw the case conference as likely to create an overreaction and increase pressures on the parent to no good effect. She was determined that the conference would not alter the approach taken by the social services department to the management of the case.

Such a strong viewpoint was rarely articulated, but particularly in the more moderate cases there was an underlying feeling that the child abuse system provided an unnecessarily clumsy response. Undoubtedly also there was an element of self interest in such views as social workers were keen not only to protect their clients, but also their own professional autonomy and control over a case. Nevertheless much concern was expressed about the stigmatic and painful effects on clients of being exposed to such a procedure.

However, in the bulk of cases in the study, social workers did adhere to the system and follow procedures closely, taking parents and children to hospital for examination often in quite stressful circumstances, and in some cases, with threats of violence against them. Most social workers in the study who had to carry out such initial investigations adopted a direct approach as exemplified in such comments as –

All injuries go straight to hospital.

We lay it on the line that its not an area in which we have discretion.

This was despite the fact that the procedural guidelines recommended the use where necessary of an indirect approach to the process –

To facilitate referral, plausible reasons e.g. 'we must find out how he bruises so easily', may be used.

Such an approach can be ultimately humiliating and distressing for the family referred. One parent went through a large part of the process without knowing definitely that there was suspicion of child abuse –

They said they were going to have a case conference – they never said

when it was going to be. They just said they were going to have a case
conference to try and find out why they think the bruising occurred.
So I thought it was a medical thing. I didn't know it was because they
thought he was getting battered.

To be in such ignorance at this stage of investigation was rare and
indeed most families were more fully informed of the reasons why
their children were being medically examined. Judging from
comments by parents they preferred a direct approach and to know
where they stood.

Medical Examination

As mentioned before 18 of the 25 cases were taken to hospital for
medical examination. Place of safety orders were used in 5 of these
cases as recommended by the procedural guidelines in instances
where parents refused to co-operate. In 2 of these cases the parents
had removed children from hospital against the advice of the
medical staff and in one they had refused social workers access to the
house. In the other 2 cases there was no immediate risk to the child
because the parents were not resistant to the action taken. Both were
cases of more serious abuse, however, and there was some fear that
the parents would become more opposed to the official response
later on. In one case the paediatrician concerned was of the belief
that all cases of suspected child abuse should be protected by place of
safety orders. In 2 cases the threat of a place of safety order was used
to ensure that parents agreed to their child staying in hospital.

Of the 18 children who received medical examinations, 9 stayed in
hospital until a case conference had been held and then returned
home (having spent between three and seven days in hospital). Five
went to foster homes or relatives after a stay in hospital, and on to a
foster-home after a medical examination. In only 2 cases was the
length of hospitalization medically warranted. The emphasis was
on the protection of children. Somewhat anomalously, 2 children
were allowed to go home straight after hospital examination,
though there was no less suspicion about abuse in these cases than
in the rest.

Siblings of the Abused Children

The question of what action should be taken with regard to siblings was not clearly tackled in the procedural guidelines. The advice given was that 'if one child is shown to have been abused, all other children in the family must be reviewed and, if necessary, examined as a matter of urgency'. As a consequence social work practice varied – as far as any pattern could be discerned, in more serious cases of abuse to an individual child, siblings were more likely to be medically examined as well and/or removed from the home. In one case where a baby aged 18 months received severe bruising to the face, the remaining 5 children (up to the ages of 10) were all removed from the home on place of safety orders despite there being no medical evidence of ill-treatment or neglect. Overall there were 11 cases involving siblings. In all but one of these it was clear that some consideration had been given to their safety, but formal medical checks had not been systematically applied to ensure this.

Pre-case conference activity

Case conferences in general took place between 3 days and a week after the initial referral (see next chapter). Most of the key social workers used this time to explain the system to the parents, to gather information and, in cases not already known, to try and assess what was happening within a family. However, given the short space of time and the degree of confusion and conflict surrounding some of the cases it was difficult to achieve a great deal. There was much variety. In one case a medical social worker worked at developing an in-depth psycho-social assessment of the family using lengthy interviews and the effects of the crisis to bring about some self-realization. A similar approach was adopted by another medical social worker. However, most assessments were not as detailed or as theoretically-based as these. In many cases, clients argued that their children had not been abused and this dominated discussions. In some cases, key workers were unavailable during this period, and those standing in for them tended not to intervene in any great depth. Most social workers stated that they had explained the system to their clients during this period. However, in 5 cases no information was given to clients about a conference being held – 3 of these were neglect cases. In these instances the parents remained unaware of events until after case conferences and only when they were informed of decisions afterwards did they realize they had taken place. In 4 cases it was apparent that the social workers went to very great lengths to explain how the system worked, who would be present at the case conferences, the issues likely to be discussed etc. Notably in all 4 of these cases, parents attended at the end of the conference to be informed of decisions reached and to be asked their points of view. In 11 cases, the period between the referral and the conference was also used for gathering information about the incident of abuse. Again there was considerable variety regarding the amount of detail sought. In general social workers did not probe too deeply. In a small number of cases, conflict between parents and the authorities was so great around this time that nothing could be achieved. In one case of severe neglect resulting in the removal on a place of safety order of the 2 children concerned, there was no contact at all with the parents during this period and in a second case the male parent threatened social workers with violence. In these circumstances no assessment other than reporting these responses could be made. It should be pointed out that assessment was also being made by other personnel at this time, particularly by nursing staff in cases where children (and parents) stayed in hospital.

Only 4 social workers had arrived at a clear view of what they wanted the outcome of the conference to be before it was held. Most social workers were prepared to be guided by the conference itself. In the case of overchastisement previously referred to in detail, the senior social worker was determined that the case conference would not alter the way in which the case was to be handled afterwards and she warded off any suggestion that the child in question be registered. In two other cases, both of physical abuse, social workers were keen to ensure that these incidents should not lead to an overreaction. In the fourth case the situation was reversed. This was a case of sexual abuse which the social worker felt was being played down by other agencies, particularly the police. She lobbied one of the principal social workers specializing in child abuse prior to the case conference in order to get her view endorsed.

The Family's view of being at the receiving end

How did the families themselves experience being investigated for child abuse? In all 10 were interviewed, 8 where physical abuse was suspected, (the other two were cases of neglect and sexual abuse). All, as one would expect, found the experience traumatic and distressing. Four of these families saw the social workers who visited them at the time of the referral to be either patronizing or authoritarian, whereas 4 felt that social workers had been helpful or supportive to them at a very difficult time. In 7 of the cases, the children stayed in hospital. In 3 cases the mothers stayed in hospital with their children – in the remaining 4 it was not clear whether they were offered the choice. One mother was barred from seeing her child. Nearly all these patients found the questioning of the hospital doctors at the initial medical examination hard to cope with. Those that stayed in the hospital felt stigmatized – they knew *they* were being observed and checked, a point brought home to one mother who wished to take her child for a walk round the hospital grounds in accordance with the practice of other mothers, and was refused. The worst experiences, however, were reserved for the 3 sets of these 10 parents whom the police were summoned to investigate. All were taken to the police station – 2 were kept in cells – and according to them, harshly interrogated. One described his and his wife's treatment as follows –

> All we got was every now and then the window would open and I don't know who it was, a sergeant, I think – you could only see his head. He'd say, 'Why don't you own up? One of you did it'. 'I've done nothing'. I said. 'Come on now, make it easier on yourself. Just one of you – say you did it. Go on. Say you did', then close the window and that's all we got.

These parents were prosecuted, but the case was finally dismissed. No prosecutions took place in the other 2 cases. In all the police investigated 13 of the total sample of 25 cases and made prosecutions in two. While they were involved in all of the serious cases of abuse it was not clear why at the moderate end of the scale some families were investigated and others were not.

Finally, 2 of the parents complained that they had not received any information about what was happening – the case of one parent has already been described. Another parent had not been informed that her children had been made the subjects of place of safety orders. It was clear that in the confusion of the investigation many parents even in cases where social workers insisted that they had given information, did not recollect this happening.

Conclusions

In the introduction to this chapter the divergent views of Parton[8] and Dingwall *et al.*[9] concerning the child abuse system were considered. In this conclusion consideration will be given to how far the data on child abuse investigation supports either view and then some general comments on social worker practice at this stage of child abuse work will be offered.

Dingwall *et al.*[10] in their study found that front-line workers with families tended not to bring cases into the open unless forced to by the fact that other agencies became involved. Such a view was confirmed by some of the findings in this study. It was notable that home visitors, such as social workers and health visitors, did not initiate investigations into any of the 25 case-study cases. Yet 13 of these were 'active' cases known to social services departments at the time of the alleged incident of abuse. In a small number of these cases social workers considered that processing them through the child abuse system was unnecessary. Group discussions with social workers confirmed the view that there was an informal screening of cases, particularly those considered to be ones of moderate abuse where social workers were already involved, and that some of these were kept out of the system. Dingwall *et al.* attribute this and other processes in the child abuse system to a rule of optimism which as I have explained in note 5 is not considered to be a preference on the part of social workers for 'seeing the best in people', but stems from the requirements of our liberal democratic society to intervene into families only with great care. In this study during the investigative stages of intervention social workers showed a preference for keeping families out of the system where possible but the reasons given for such a preference were that such action might lead a) to an overreaction to families' problems and b) to social workers' losing control of situations which they felt most suited to deal with because of their close knowledge of the families concerned.

The 25 case-study cases were all ones which for a variety of reasons passed through the informal screening stage just described. As has been suggested before the sample as a whole was skewed to the more serious end of the spectrum of child abuse and there was generally less equivocation in such cases. Where it fell to social workers to be involved in the early stages of intervention in these cases they followed the procedural guidelines closely and ensured in the case of physical abuse that children were medically examined. According to the small group of clients interviewed, some social workers managed to handle the authority situation that resulted in a humane and understanding way; others adopted an authoritarian or patronizing approach. Most social workers felt they had adequately explained to families why they were taking the action that they were and what was likely to happen. However, some clients felt they were poorly informed about what was taking place. A minority felt they had received poor treatment particularly from the police and to a less extent from the medical and nursing staff. All clients felt highly stigmatized by the process. There is no doubt that the stage of entry into the child abuse system is a painful one for clients. If a 'rule of optimism' is operating at this stage then it is doing so very unobtrusively as far as those at the receiving end are concerned. Despite the efforts of some social workers and other health and welfare professionals to humanize the process the system at this stage fits far more closely with Parton's view of a harsh and authoritarian process that front-line workers are forced to implement.

Overall, therefore, evidence from this stage of social work intervention suggests that there is some support for those who see the system as rather liberally operated and also for those who see it as a harsh instrument of intervention into family life. Much depends on value stances in the child protection/rights of families debate[11] and from whose point of view the system is observed.

Social Work Practice Issues

With regard to social work practice issues the following points stand out –

1. Social workers' perceptions of the child abuse system vary, but many are suspicious of the way in which it operates for the reasons already outlined. As will be seen this negative perception, particularly with regard to less serious cases, is voiced again in the next chapter which deals with case conferences. The system is clearly seen by some to be oppressive and in certain cases leads to practices which are dysfunctional as far as the formal aims of the enterprise are concerned i.e. social workers carry out informal screening of some cases. It may well be that the system should recognize and accept the inevitability of this by allowing front-line workers more discretion at this stage to decide whether to ask for case conferences or not. This would clearly have some implications for the training and orientation of such workers and also flies in the face of current trends. Nevertheless, the findings of this study with regard to this early investigative stage suggest the need for some

changes. These ideas will be further developed in the concluding chapter.

2. While recognizing the conflictual nature of encounters between social workers and families at this stage of intervention the findings particularly from the parents' interviews suggest that greater consideration needs to be given to explaining as clearly as possible what is happening and is likely to happen as far as the social worker knows. Practice varied from close attention to such explanation to avoidance of being direct (which was partially encouraged by the procedural guidelines). Parents were clearly in such turmoil that they were less likely to receive information than in normal circumstances. Social work practitioners (even if they are distressed themselves) need to recognize this and concentrate hard on giving clear and accurate information. Some consideration could be given to the use of written information about the powers of the local authority and the process which is gone through.

3. Parents felt that they received harsh treatment from some professionals – this included social workers, the police, hospital doctors and nurses. There is no way of calculating the extent of this factor and judging from some parental comments, observation at case conferences and the views of social workers much was done in many cases to alleviate the harsher aspects of child abuse investigation. Nevertheless, it is important that the response to child abuse does not become over-emotional and too judgemental. Even if only one agency responds in this way this is likely to colour the client's impression of other agencies as well and have negative consequences with regard to future work.[12] Clearly this is a problem for all agencies and training could overcome some of these difficulties.

4. A final point of concern was that regarding the immediate protection of children prior to a case conference. It is accepted practice following the work of Kempe[13] to ensure the placement of a child at risk in a protective environment (with or without the parent(s)). This practice was followed in all but two of the physical abuse cases (no clear reason could be seen for these exceptions). In some cases there was little doubt that such action was necessary. However, in others the risks did not seem so great. Some parents were allowed to stay with children in hospital, though, as has been indicated, this was not always a pleasant experience for them; others were not offered the opportunity. Some consideration does need to be given to whether Kempe's 'rule' needs to be interpreted more flexibly and to ensuring that non-stigmatic environments are available allowing parents and children to be together unless there are clear reasons for not taking such a course of action. There was more uncertainty (and no clear guidelines) with regard to the protection of siblings and in most cases this resulted in a more flexible approach.

Certainly no siblings of the case-study children came to harm during this stage even though most remained with their parents.

Notes

1. The exception to this was the case of 3 year old Darryn Clarke. In this case, the relatives of Darryn were concerned because his mother, a lone parent, had left her home to live with a man in another part of Liverpool at an address unknown to them, and on one occasion when she visited them they were shocked at Darryn's appearance – he had some facial bruising, a badly cropped hair cut and was uncharacteristically quiet and withdrawn. After a period in which Darryn's mother had not visited again, the relatives became increasingly concerned and went to the local police station to see if they could secure help in tracing him. However, the response to the concern of Darryn's relatives by the police and other agencies who later became involved was not as urgent as with hindsight it should have been. Two factors particularly contributed to this – the fact that there was no known history of abuse and the thought that the relatives might be overreacting. (The situation was not helped by the fact that these events took place over the Christmas period). It took just over three weeks after the visit to the police station to find Darryn by which time he had been so severely abused by his mother's cohabitee that he died soon afterwards. This case in particular sensitized agencies to the need to respond quickly and with urgency to any allegations of abuse, but did not lead to the introduction of mandatory reporting.
See pages 10–44 DHSS, (1979), The Report of the Committee of Inquiry into the Actions of the Authorities and Agencies Relating to Darryn James Clarke. HMSO.
2. 'A Child in Trust'. The Report of the Panel of Inquiry into the Circumstances Surrounding the death of Jasmine Beckford (1985). London Borough of Brent p. 145.
3. N. Parton, (1985), *The Politics of Child Abuse*, p. 127 Macmillan.
4. R. Dingwall, J. Eekelaar and T. Murray, (1983), *The Protection of Children* B. Blackwell, (p. 79).
5. This term 'rule of optimism' has led to some confusion. Close reading of the text of the work of Dingwall *et al.* makes it clear that social workers and front-line workers do not arbitrarily select to be optimistic about suspected cases of child abuse. Drawing on the work of Donzelot (*The Policing of Families*, Hutchinson, 1979) they argue that such an approach is determined by the requirements of the liberal-democratic state which are that as far as is consonant with the well-being of children the family should not be undermined by outside intervention because of its key function in the socializing of children.
   The Beckford inquiry report takes up the notion of 'the rule of optimism' (p. 216), but sees it as something in which front-line workers have more personal choice than was intended by its original authors. The inquiry sees the

rule of optimism as a dysfunctional characteristic of the social work profession in particular and sees this as partly to blame for the behaviour of social workers in this particular case. It pays little attention to the broader social influences on intervention into family life.

6. BASW, (1978), *The Central Child Abuse Register*, paras. 2.6.11–2.6.15).
7. See H. Geach, (1983), 'Child Abuse Registers – time for a change?' (p. 53) in H. Geach and E. Szwed, *Providing Civil Justice for Children*, Edward Arnold.
8. N. Parton, (1985), op. cit.
9. R. Dingwall *et al.*, (1983), op. cit.
10. R. Dingwall *et al.*, (1983), op. cit. see p. 96 and their comments on 'the failure of containment'.
11. See L. Fox, (1982), 'Two value positions in recent child care law and practice', *British Journal of Social Work* vol. 12 no. 3.
12. For instance those families seen by the police as a result of a suspected incident of abuse assumed that they and the social services department worked closely together. This led them to be suspicious of the 'softer' approach of social workers later on.
13. See R.S. and C.H. Kempe, (1978), *Child Abuse*, Fontana.

Chapter 5

Official Decision-Making at Case Conferences

A case conference is recommended for every case involving suspected non-accidental injury to a child. In this way unilateral action will be minimised and all those who can provide information about the child and his family, have statutory responsibility for the safety of the child, or are responsible for providing services, will be brought together to reach a collective decision which takes into account the age of the child, nature of injuries and a medico-social assessment of the family and its circumstances. (DHSS guidelines on case conferences.)

There are inherent difficulties with a large body of people from diverse professional groupings. They are helpful in that you are spreading the burden. I'm not convinced that the solutions arrived at are necessarily all that helpful towards social workers in the way that they deal with cases and perceive situations.
(North City Social worker.)

Introduction

Much of the important decision-making in child abuse cases takes place in case conferences. While the DHSS circular[1] which followed the publication of the Maria Colwell inquiry report[2] can be seen as a starting point for the type of child abuse case conferences that currently exist, it should be noted that as early as 1950 the Home Office and other relevant government departments had recommended inter-agency co-ordinating committees for communicating concern about neglected and ill-treated children.[3] There is no account of how these bodies operated. However, it is probable that they were used to discuss families with children who were perceived as problematic users of a wide range of social services i.e. 'problem families',[4] whereas most child abuse conferences today are specifically concerned with incidents of abuse to children.[5]

The official functions of the case conference are as follows –

1. to establish the facts of an incident of abuse
2. to share information about the family
3. to make an assessment of the family and
4. to agree on and recommend a course of action

In theory this is a simple and straightforward task. However, in practice, there are many associated difficulties and problems. One of the major stumbling blocks is that of communication between the different professional groupings which attend conferences. Typical attenders at a case conference concerning a physically abused baby might be –

1. the chairperson
2. a senior social worker (social services department)
3. a social worker (social services department)
4. a police inspector
5. a health visitor
6. a community nursing officer
7. a medical social worker
8. a hospital doctor
9. the ward sister
10. the general practitioner
11. an NSPCC inspector

If the child had siblings of school age, we could add –

12. the school headteacher (or year tutor)
13. an educational welfare officer
14. a school nurse

If one of the parents was on probation we could add –

15. the probation officer

and depending on other circumstances we could add –

16. a nursery nurse
17. a family aide
18. a residential social worker
19. a foster parent
20. an educational psychologist
21. a psychiatrist
22. a city solicitor

Hallet and Stevenson[6] have pointed to the problems of communication that can exist at case conferences given the diversity of professional backgrounds, beliefs and responsibilities of such a varied group of people. They focus particularly on the social psychological aspects such as stereotyping between professionals which acts as a barrier to communications resulting in people hearing only what they expect to hear. Dale[7] feels that disputes between agencies which focus on their narrow concerns rather than the problem as a whole 'seriously interfere with the successful treatment and management of child abusing families'. Dingwall *et al.*'s study[8] similarly saw inter-agency differences as conspiring to reduce the probability of identifying child-mistreatment. Hence there is a growing body of evidence to suggest that case conferences as they currently operate are not achieving the tasks they were intended to achieve.

In addition to communication, a major issue is that concerning the authority that the case conference possesses over its participants. The Beckford report,[9] for instance, adopts the view that the case conference recommends and advises action. However, it goes on to confuse the issue somewhat by discussing whether recommendations should be *decisive* or not. 'We have heard it said that one of the besetting defects of case conferences is their indecisiveness. In part, that complaint stems from a misunderstanding of the role of case conferences. They do not, nor ought they to, make decisions. But, given that case conferences are advisory bodies, it may still be said that their recommendations should be decisive'. In other words they should make definite recommendations. Clearly case conferences decisions are not legally binding on individuals or agencies – some agencies, the police, for instance, maintain their right to independent action regardless of case conference decisions. However, case conference decisions in North City (as is true in many parts of the country) did have a *de facto* binding authority over social workers, because the conferences were chaired by social services personnel, who, while not being line managers, did in practice carry responsibility for the management of the child abuse system. It seems, therefore, that the case conference system has greater authority over some than others.

These and other issues will be examined throughout this chapter. Data is derived from three main sources, the general group discussions with teams of social workers, interviews with social workers who had responsibility for the 25 cases which formed the core of the study and observation of 55 case conferences from which the 25 cases were selected for more detailed analysis.

In particular social workers' views of the operation of case conferences will be considered and an attempt will be made to evaluate and provide a critique of the way in which case conferences were conducted. Finally reference will be made to clients' views about being on the receiving end of case conferences.

Case Conferences in North City

All 25 of the cases in this study became the subject of case conferences, most within a week of the initial referral.[10] Because of the way in which the research was designed (i.e. using the case conferences as the starting point) it was not possible to gauge in general the number of cases in which official investigations of abuse were initiated, but not referred on to case conferences. The impression gained was that once a child had been referred to hospital as a suspected case of abuse he or she was likely to be the subject of a case conference subsequently. In most physical abuse cases the decision was reached almost automatically between the medical and social work staff of the hospitals. It was rare for social workers already working with families to call case conferences on these families themselves – however, as was pointed out in the previous chapter, most accepted the need for them to take place.

Eighteen of the initial case conferences took place in one or other of the two children's hospitals. As indicated in Chapter 3, just over a third of the cases were ones of moderate physical abuse and over a third were ones of serious physical abuse. There were 3 cases of sexual abuse, three cases of physical neglect and one unborn baby case where the mother had killed a previous child.

Numbers attending

The numbers attending the case conferences varied between 8 and 20, the average being approximately 11. The 'serious' abuse cases generally had the highest number of attenders. Table 5.1 gives details of those who attended the 25 case conferences.

It is notable that the police and social services department representatives attended all conferences, the police often sending 2 officers, and social services 3. Health visitors were much less likely to be accompanied by senior staff than were social workers. General practitioner attendance was low as was that of hospital consultants. No legal advice was available at any of the initial conferences.[11] The NSPCC attended if they had prior involvement with a family and this was true of other agencies.

Table 5.1 Personnel attending 25 cases conferences

	Number attending		Number attending
Social Worker	38	Senior nursing officer	4
Senior Social Worker	22	Clinic doctor	2
Police 35	35	G.P.	4
Hospital Social Worker	14	School Nurse	9
Consultant	3	School doctor	4
Registrar & other	23	School teacher	13
Nursing staff	4	Education Welfare Officer	3
Health visitor	20	Matron (nursery)	8
Probation Officer	6	NSPCC	6
City Solicitors	0	Foster parent	1
Miscellaneous	5	Chairperson	25
Secretary	25		

Total 274 (average 10.96)

Duration of Case Conferences

The conferences lasted for between 30 minutes and one and a half hours. The average length of time per conference was one hour. Most conferences adopted a similar format. Initially, the chairperson checked on factual details such as the spelling of names, dates of birth and addresses. Secondly focus was placed on the incident of abuse and the period immediately following. If possible those who were present at that time contributed at this point. The third stage was devoted to assessing the family. This stage included past history as known to the various agencies and current reaction to the abuse investigation. The final stage was that of decision-making and allocating tasks.

Available disposals

The case conference had available to it four possible disposals. The first was to take no further action. The second was to allocate a case to one of the agencies for help and monitoring (or if a social worker was already involved to confirm the status quo). The third disposal was to place a child's name on the central child abuse register and allocate the case to one of the agencies for help and monitoring and the final disposal was to recommend care proceedings. Usually in such cases children's names were placed on the register as well. This range of disposals acted in practice as a form of tariff.

Table 5.2 sets out the diposals used in the 25 cases.

Table 5.2 Outcome of 25 case conferences

Disposal	Number	Per cent
1. No further action	0	–
2. SSD or other agency to monitor	7	28
3. Registration and SSD or other agency to monitor	11	44
4. Care proceedings or Wardship	6	24
5. Other*	1	4
	25	100

*This case concerned alleged sexual abuse against two children by the foster father. They were already in care at the time of the alleged incident and were removed to a residential home.

As has been indicated in an earlier chapter, these cases were not typical of the whole sample of child abuse cases dealt with by the system. It was more representative as a whole of the serious end.

Case Conference Norms

Analysing events in the case conference i.e. why certain decisions were taken and how these decisions were reached was problematic. This was largely because there were few explicit rules or criteria in operation. There was no formal discussion of criteria for estimating degrees of risk and little overt debate regarding the evaluation of the relative seriousness of different forms of abuse. It was assumed that there was an agreement over norms, and, as a result, this assumption had a powerful normative effect. It was rare to observe open conflict at case conferences and most decisions were reached with apparent consensus. This was particularly true in cases of serious injury or neglect in which there was reasonable evidence that abuse had taken place. In the more problematic grey area cases there were more signs of conflict, albeit of a curtailed rather than full-blown form.

The following case gives some flavour of the type and form of disagreement that was in evidence. In this particular case, a two-month old child had been referred by his parents to the hospital with a bruised and bleeding nose. The child had, according to the parents, fallen on to it's face from a rocker-chair. Medical evidence, based on an assessment of the injuries, pointed to the feasibility of such an explanation. However, medical records of this child's two year old sister showed that in the eighteen months prior to this incident she had been treated in hospital on two separate occasions with a fractured skull and a dislocated elbow. In addition nursery records showed that during the same period bruises were observed on her by nurses.

The police inspector at the conference, who was not a regular attender, was the only one to voice concern at this string of injuries. 'Maybe I'm a bit cynical, but it begins to look more than an accidental series of events. It's more than one would expect'.

However, he was firmly rebutted by the chairperson who stated that on each occasion the parents had given reasonable explanations for the occurrence of the injuries. The inspector, clearly disgruntled, later complained that the police should have been notified of this case immediately after the medical examination. The hospital registrar's response to this was that the injury was not considered serious enough to warrant such a referral. The inspector's last effort to assert his viewpoint on this case was to request that the police be notified at an early stage if there were any further injuries. The chairperson, by now somewhat exasperated, retorted that the police were only involved if a case was considered to be serious. With that the conflict ended.

This police inspector broke the no-conflict norm, but by and large it was preserved and most decisions were reached with little overt conflict. Occasionally a vote was taken to decide whether a child's name should be placed on the abuse register. However, even when such a course of action was resorted to it was rare for there to be a dissenting voice.

The fact that the police inspector was, as mentioned above, not a regular attender at case conferences may explain his persistence in disagreeing with everyone. By and large, there was a group of regular attenders at conferences in North City. Medical social workers and more senior hospital doctors attended several case conferences a year. The police generally used the same officers to attend conferences.

As a result they and the chairperson had regular contact and developed a working relationship. Other front-line professionals attended conferences far less regularly. Senior social workers by being responsible for a group of social workers attended somewhat more regularly. Nevertheless there was an insider/outsider split. In addition the insiders were normally high-ranking police officers or hospital doctors, thus having greater professional status than the outsiders as well, and so were at a considerable advantage. This on occasions led to experience prevailing over logic. As a result it was rare for outsiders to question or challenge accepted wisdoms. It is perhaps notable that in the example of conflict outlined above the outsider who challenged the norm was a policeman of relatively high status.

There were 2 further influences on the 'no-conflict' norm. The first was the 'risky' nature of child abuse work (by which I mean risk to the professionals) and the second was the time-limit placed on the decision-making process. Because child abuse is perceived as a high-risk business it was rare for individual professionals to take a strong line on a case at the case conference. If anyone did then generally they had their way. This did not mean that 'risky' decisions were not taken – as will be seen, they were. However, it did mean that there was generally little conflict about the final decision reached. This was aided by the effect of time-limits which while not specified, operated at an implicit level. On average, as mentioned above, most decisions were reached within an hour. Often the final decision seemed to be rushed to fit in with this time-limit. Occasionally decisions were deferred to allow for further information to be obtained. There were pressures against this – a) it entailed reconvening all the professionals within a short space of time, a costly and time-consuming exercise and b) it meant that in many cases parents and children remained separated for a longer period than might otherwise have been necessary.

All these factors, therefore, led to much greater consensus within the conference than might be expected. Clearly the dynamics of such meetings tend for the various reasons suggested to push towards conformity.

Social Workers' Views of Case Conference

Group discussions with social workers, however, revealed considerable dissatisfaction with the case conference system. The most commonly voiced criticisms were as follows –

1. too many people attended.
2. too much weight was place on the contributions of those with little responsibility for or knowledge of the cases concerned.
3. certain personnel, particularly the police, dominated conferences.
4. Regular attenders (usually identified as the police or hospital doctors) held an unfair advantage at conferences.
5. Not enough care was taken to ensure that non-factual and emotive comments were eliminated.

The underlying themes to all these views were concerns regarding power, control and responsibility. Many social workers felt that they had prime responsibility for dealing with families who were subjects of the case conferences (and this was particularly acutely felt with regard to already 'known' cases) yet they perceived that they had little power or influence over the decision-making process itself. As one social worker put it –

> It always worries me at case conferences that the only agency who is going to deal with the situation if removal is decided upon is the social services – no other agency. Because they don't have to deal with the follow-through they, therefore, will take that step more easily than we will, because we know the problems of kids in care, but we're the only agency that knows that – that's why we're hanging back much more and that's why we're often the ones in the position of saying no.

Many social workers considered themselves to be 'outsiders' at case conferences and that the police and hospital consultants had an unfair advantage over them in terms of status and regularity of attendance. The situation, as they saw it, was exacerbated by the fact that in over 90 per cent of the cases they assumed the key worker role and had to implement the decisions reached, which was particularly problematic if they did not entirely agree with them. In addition, many social workers felt they had a special claim to influence in the case conference because only they were fully cognisant of the care system and its deficiencies. As a result they tended to weigh up the risks of leaving children at home against those of removing them to substitute care. Other agencies were perceived as seeing this approach as evidence of softness or equivocation on the part of social workers because of their more optimistic view of the benefits of substitute care.

These were the most common views voiced in group discussion with social workers. Some, however, did point to the fact that case conference decisions provided a form of collective security. This was particularly true in cases of serious abuse where statutory action was being considered. In these circumstances social workers' views with regard to case conferences were far more favourable.

These generally critical views of the case conference system were not entirely born out by the experiences of the social workers dealing with the 25 cases selected for closer study nor by observations of the 55 conferences from which the sample was selected. Data from these sources will be used in what follows to consider the specific complaints raised by social workers in the group discussions i.e. that too many people attended conferences, that social work contributions were not given enough weight, that other agency professionals particularly the police and hospital doctors had an unfair advantage and that a good deal of unsubstantiated and emotive criticism was made of parents. In addition further consideration will be given to the decision-making process i.e. what factors influenced the outcomes.

Too many attenders

Reference has already been made to the numbers attending the case conferences in which the study cases featured. The average attendance number was 11 and the social workers dealing with these cases did not perceive them to be over-attended. A check was made (in all 55 conferences observed) of how many case conference attenders actually did not say anything throughout the meetings. This can only be seen as a rough indicator of the necessity of their attendance as part of the function of going to case conferences is to receive information. However, approximately 10 per cent of those attending made no verbal contribution. Twenty per cent of police attenders said nothing and 20 per cent of the health visitors. In the former case this is not surprising as they attended all conferences regardless of their involvement or likely involvement in a case. It is more surprising with regard to the health visitors as they always had some direct involvement with children under five as a justification of their need to attend. A general impression formed from observing conferences was that in many of them agencies sent more than one representative, particularly the police and social services, as a matter of course, or purely for support/strength in numbers purposes. It was felt that greater consideration should have been given to balancing the importance of inviting all those with a legitimate concern in a case with the need for good communication which can be hampered by the presence of large numbers of people.[12]

The Impact of Social Workers' Contributions
With regard to the weight given to social work contributions, most of the social workers in the case-study felt that they had been given 'a fair hearing' at the case conferences. Four of the 25 were dissatisfied at the decision reached in the conference. In three of these cases it was felt that the decision reached was more severe than it should have been. In the fourth case, the social worker came away from the conference feeling unsure about what decision had been reached.

The Impact of Others' Contributions
Fourteen social workers were critical of the contribution of personnel from other agencies. In particular, the police were singled out for criticism, not always, as one would expect, for supporting over-intrusive strategies, but in the case of two allegations of sexual abuse, for being unwilling to intervene. Complaints centred more on style than content – the police were seen by social workers to lack sensitivity in this area of work. Criticisms of other agency personnel were mainly around the theme that they wanted drastic responses to situations that in the eyes of the social workers did not warrant them. Less frequently voiced was the criticism that other agencies' unwillingness to take a definite stance precluded the possibility of taking more intrusive action.[13]

Emotive Criticisms of Parents
Direct observation of case conferences did confirm that, as the social workers in the group discussions pointed out, there was a good deal of emotive and unsubstantiated criticism of families. However, not all of such criticism, came from workers other than social workers. The most frequent references were to –

1. late rising
   e.g. 'They're never up till mid-afternoon'.

2. poor standards of hygiene
   e.g. 'The cleanest thing I found in the house on Saturday night was the Afghan hound'.

3. devious characteristics
   e.g. 'She is quick enough to make up stories – she's bright enough for that. I felt she was quite manipulative. I felt she was used to conning people left, right and centre'.

4. immaturity or low intelligence.
   e.g. 'He's one of life's casualties – not very bright. He went to ESN school. He's easily led'.

It was rare that comments such as these were objected to or that someone asked for factual verification. How influential such comments were in the final decision-making was not apparent. There is little doubt that one of the purposes they served was that of a safety valve for the pressures, anxieties, fears and anger of the workers involved. In cases where there were good grounds for believing that serious abuse had taken place they did serve to support the view that the family in question was morally inferior anyway which could help explain their apparently cruel actions.

Some of the criticisms raised in the group discussions were, therefore, confirmed by the views of the social workers in the case-study and by the findings from observation of the 55 case conferences. However, the criticisms voiced by the case-study social workers were less extreme than those voiced in the social work teams. One reason for this may be a methodological one. Dingwall,[14] drawing on research into the practice of health visiting discusses the self-enhancing function of 'atrocity stories' for professional groups, particularly regarding situations where they interact with other professionals with whom they compete for status. To some extent the teams of social workers, may have focused only on the difficult and, to them, anomalous experiences encountered in case conferences. It may be, therefore, that dissatisfaction with the system was not as widespread as these group discussions initially suggested. Nevertheless, there is clearly unease on the part of social workers about case conferences. There are pitfalls and dangers associated with them which affect the way in which they are perceived and responded to. It is highly likely that other professional groups share some of these anxieties and beliefs. In Hallett and Stevenson's study,[15] other agencies perceived social workers to wield considerable power at case conferences. Whatever the case it is clear that despite the apparent lack of overt conflict at case conferences there are a considerable number of difficulties felt by social workers and others in their operation.

Use of Theory/Research

There was little direct reference to child abuse literature or theories in the case conferences. However, implicit in many decisions was the notion that a combination of external stress factors and poor childhood experiences on the part of the parents themselves were the main causes of abuse. Stress factors were rarely directly referred to. Deprived childhood theories were used in a loose way to justify a belief that a parent had injured a child in the absence of firm evidence. However, in one case evidence of deprived background was used to prevent a case conference from reacting too harshly. In this case a 9 month old baby suffered a fractured skull and the parental explanation was very vague. The father of the child was currently in the care of the local authority and the mother had previously been in care. This information was not used at the conference as a cause for concern, rather the opposite. The medical social worker preempted such a stance by stating, 'The mother is worried that being in care et cetera will go against her'. In this case the disadvantage of having been in care acted in favour of the parents. It was rare to hear such factors as birth difficulties[16] or critical path analysis[17] used as indicators of potential abuse situations – however, such circumstances were on occasions described. Particularly in the physical abuse cases much of the conference was devoted to consideration of medical and legal factors, supporting the finding of Dingwall *et al.*[18] that an important function of the case conference is to decide whether or not a case can be 'framed' for court action.

Care Proceedings Decisions

Only 6 of the 25 study cases were referred for court action. Four were cases of physical abuse and 2 of neglect, (one a serious case of malnutrition, the other a case of inadequate parenting due to alcohol addiction on the part of the mother). The latter case was ultimately dropped and this was the only one of the six over which there was obvious disagreement about a future course of action. In four of these cases there had been a history of abuse and in all but one there had been ongoing social work involvement as a result of concern for the children prior to the current incident. While the numbers are small the findings would suggest in line with Dingwall[19] *et al.*'s research findings and those of Parker *et al.*'s[20] that care proceedings is an end-of-the-line activity entered into after attempts to manage a situation or to achieve change by voluntary means have failed.

Avoiding Care Proceedings

Indeed there was considerable pressure to avoid care porceedings. In 9 cases, conferences ended with uncertainty as to how an injury had been caused. In three of these cases the injuries were serious and in two others there had been several instances of suspicious moderate abuse. There was a marked tendency to take an optimistic view of such situations along the lines suggested by Dingwall *et al.*[21]

The following example illustrates features of this approach.

An investigation into a swollen leg injury on a 5 month old baby resulted in the discovery (by means of x-ray) of a previous injury in which 5 ribs had been cracked. Both parents denied having inflicted such an injury. Among explanations offered for the cause of the injury was that it might have happened as a result of the baby's 4 year old sister sitting on him. While there was considerable concern about the parents and the situation they were in, little direct attention was given to the injury to the ribs, and there was a considerable push towards accepting that the injury was not the result of deliberate abuse.

The medical social worker, for instance, focused on the mother's reaction to being told about this previous injury – 'She's either an exceedingly good actress or she was very surprised about the ribs'. She stressed how co-operative the parents had been during the investigation. The health visitor supported such a view – 'They're not the best parents in the world, but I was surprised about the ribs. As far as non-accidental injury goes they're not a family I would say would cause a child an injury'.

Significantly the hospital registrar did not feel able to be definite about the cause of the rib injury, and, therefore, no conflict arose. Token consideration was given to the possibility of care proceedings and the final decision, without further reference to the rib injury, was to place the child's name on the central abuse register and allocate the case to a social worker. This approach characterized all of the 9 cases referred to – in 5 cases the children's name were placed on the register and in 4 they were allocated for ongoing social worker intervention.

Register Decisions

There seemed to be a lack of consistency in the decisions whether or not to place the child's name on the abuse register. Eleven of the 25 cases were registered and 8 were not. In the observer's judgement there was cause for as much concern in 4 of the non-registered cases as there was in the 11 cases registered. Similarly there were 3 cases which were registered which did not seem to be any more risky than the non-registered cases. As an example of the latter case, one woman, a single parent, had bruised her seven year old child having lost her temper with her when getting her ready for bed. She sought help from the social services department openly admitting that she had struck her child in anger. Despite a willingness to accept social work intervention and the fact that there was no history of abuse the child's name was placed on the register. The deciding factor was the mother's admission. This was proof of the occurrence of abuse and, therefore, the department had to be seen to respond to it. Little discussion took place regarding the degree of risk involved or as to whether seeking help was to be seen as an indicator of a positive outcome over time.

This lack of consistency with regard to registration decisions was born out by an analysis of all 55 case conferences observed. (see Appendix 3). While it was generally clear why decisions were reached to undertake care proceedings, the decision whether or not to register was not clearly linked to any specific criteria. At the conferences observed use of the register created a good deal of controversy – some argued that it should be a list of children about whom concern existed regardless of whether an injury or instance of neglect was provable; others took a much more legalistic line. Some social workers were mindful of the dubious legitimacy of registers and the threat they could pose to civil liberties. The register served a variety of functions. First, it was a tangible expression of concern and satisfied people that something had been done. Secondly it attempted to rank cases in some order of assessed seriousness (though as has been indicated not always successfully). Thirdly, it had a rationing function – it was argued that registration ensured continuing social work involvement and access to scarce resources such as day nurseries which might not otherwise have been available. Fourthly, registration was occasionally favoured by the chairperson because of doubts about a social worker's competence in the field of child abuse and being on the register ensured regular reviews of the case and by implication of the social worker's practice. Both these latter practices are ethically dubious and fortunately rare, but illustrative of the variety of reasons which could be used to justify a decision to register a child's name. Such a variety of reasons for registering clearly places some doubt on the credibility to be attached to registers.

The Views of the Parents

Finally in this chapter consideration will be given to case conferences as the parents saw them. Two main issues arose out of interviews with the 10 families. The first was that concerning the right to attend case conferences and the second, a closely related issue, was about securing information about what was happening. Three out of the 10 parents felt strongly that they should have been allowed to attend conferences throughout. As one of them put it –

> I tell you one thing that really did annoy me and which I think they should make law is that we weren't allowed in the conference – I mean that conference was about me and my baby – so we should have been allowed to sit in and listen to what they all had to say. I mean, I don't think it's very nice sitting there discussing someone's whole future, someone's life, and they've got no say. I just think people have a right to know what's being said about them at case conferences.

Two of the parents definitely did not wish to attend. One said she was too frightened to go – another put it succinctly –

> I just didn't want to hear what people were saying about me.

Three of the parents spoken to said they had not been told that a case conference was going to be held. Clearly social work practice was very variable. For instance the following parent had received considerable information and reassurance about what was going to happen in the case conference.

> She said at the conference she was going to put in and ask could we have custody of the baby and she'll involve herself and check up. The medical social worker told me they were putting in that they didn't want the baby taken off me.

This mother as well as receiving these assurances was told exactly who would be at the case conference and what they would be discussing. However, not all parents received the same assurances, as the following account from another mother illustrates.

> I was sitting there and I must have smoked 40 cigarettes in the hour they were in there. I was in a terrible state. The woman social worker came out and said, 'It's all right, you can take Terry home' She said 'Everything's been sorted out. They didn't tell me what had been said or nothing.

No parent attended right through a conference. Five sets of parents from the 25 case studies attended conferences at the end. One parent found the experience of attending for the last part of the conference somewhat humiliating, but had not been helped by being poorly informed about who would be attending.

> I was embarrassed more than anything because Tracy's headmistress and Tracy's teacher were there. My head was down all the time – I was crying . . . if I'd been told they were going to be there, fair enough. I would have been all right, prepared.

This issue about client participation at child abuse case conferences is clearly a thorny one and has been the subject of much discussion recently.[22] While those concerned with family rights are unequivocal about the fact that parents should have the right to attend such conferences there have been several arguments put forward by the professionals involved against such attendance. The most frequently voiced arguments for such a policy are as follows –

1. that case conferences are not decision-making bodies, but consultation meetings of professional workers. On these grounds parental attendance can only be justified if all professionals deem it to be a good thing. If professionals do not agree on this then it is fair and legitimate that parents be excluded.
2. that professionals might be inhibited from sharing important information about families if they were present, thus diminishing the likelihood of making effective recommendations.
3. that parents might incriminate themselves at case conferences.
4. that parents would find such conferences threatening and difficult to cope with.

The social workers dealing with the 25 case-study cases were asked their views on this issue. Only 4 felt that parents should have been present throughout conferences, all on the grounds of civil rights. Twelve of the social workers were opposed to parents attending conferences. Most of these expressed concern that parents would not be able to cope with the threatening situation that they felt such conferences to create. To some extent this was a surprising finding in that many social workers in group discussions had seemed very aware of issues concerning parental rights. In practice, however, most felt less concerned about their rights of attendance and more concerned to protect them from being hurt. Very few of the social workers saw parental attendance at a case conference as having any beneficial effect as far as future intervention was concerned.

Conclusion

The findings concerning child abuse conferences are as follows. The overall picture is one of underlying confusion and disagreement which rarely evidenced itself in open conflict. This confusion should not be seen as surprising or as confirmation of poor practice. If one takes a wide range of ill-defined and problematic phenomena such as those that come under the heading of child abuse and asks a wide range of health, welfare and police officials to come together and agree on a course of action then one can expect a certain lack of consistency in decisions reached. If we add to this a lack of specific training for child abuse work together with inadequate resources and the contradictions of a liberal society which expects equal weight to be given to child protection and the rights of families to be self-determining, then the difficulties increase. The system does sort out cases in a rough and ready way. However, the logic of this is not always apparent to the outside observer except in the more glaringly serious cases of abuse or neglect. A good deal of decision-making is based on implicit norms and on the judgement of professionals who have seen the individuals concerned and made assessments on the basis of these perceptions. Another important factor is the role of the chairperson who by seeing a range of cases develops his or her own rating scale. It should not, therefore, be assumed that case conferences do not have a logic of their own. They serve a variety of functions such as case management, protection of professionals, an observable official response to the problem of child abuse and a rough compromise between the rights of parents and the protection of children at risk. At the same time they create many dysfunctions of the kind that the views of the social work teams pointed to. Whether or not this situation can or should be improved upon will be considered in the final chapter when the implications of this study for practice and policy will be considered.

With regard to those on the receiving end, there is little doubt that the case conference, as the immediately preceding period of investigation, is a difficult and anxiety-provoking event for parents. Until the debate concerning parental participation at such conferences reaches any conclusions about rights of attendance there is bound to be confusion and conflict over this issue. Generally with regard to communication about conferences parents had a variety of experiences – some were given much information and reassurance, others received little or none. The social workers' views about client participation pointed to social workers in practice adopting a rather paternalistic stance, assuming that they knew what was best for clients. What most of the small number of parents stressed was the fear of what might happen and a feeling of things suddenly being beyond their control. Certainly those who received good information about what was likely to happen and how the system operated experienced some anxiety-reduction. It should be apparent that in most cases open communication has beneficial consequences both in terms of immediate and long-term gains. The issue of full participation by parents in case conference merits closer consideration both for these reasons and those of parental rights.

Notes

1. DHSS letter (LASSL 80)4) 'Child Abuse Central Register Systems', 1980.
2. DHSS (1974) Report of the Committee of Inquiry into the Care and Supervision Provided in Relation to Maria Colwell. HMSO.
3. Joint Circular from the Home Office, Ministry of Health and Ministry of Education, on Children Neglected or Ill-treated in their own homes, 1950, HMSO.
4. See A.F. Philp and N. Timms, (1962), *The problem of the 'Problem Family'*, Family Service Unit.
5. It may well be that the same types of cases are being considered by the child abuse case conference system as was previously considered by the co-ordinating Committees. The only difference may be that a specific instance of abuse is focused on as the official reason for investigation. In other words problem families may have been redefined as families in which child abuse take place. If this is the case then these 'problem families' form only part of the total population considered. The net has been spread much more widely than it was before 1974.
6. C. Hallett and O. Stevenson, (1980), *Child Abuse: Aspects of Interprofessional Communication*, Allen & Unwin.
7. P. Dale, (1984), 'The Danger Within Ourselves', 1.3.84. *Community Care*.
8. R. Dingwall, J. Eekelaar and T. Murray, (1983), *The Protection of Children*, Blackwell.
9. *A Child in Trust*, The Report of the Panel of Inquiry into the Circumstances surrounding the death of Jasmine Beckford (1985). London Borough of Brent, p. 251.
10. The shortest time-gap between initial referral and case conference was one day and the longest one month. In cases of physical abuse where children were detained in hospital, often separated from their parents, conferences were held within a week of admission. There was considerable concern to expedite the system in such cases. To some extent this time-pressure led to hasty decision-making that occasionally precluded full assessment of the situation. Reconvening conferences rarely occurred because of this pressure.

11. The comments of the Jasmine Beckford report (op. cit.) about who should attend conferences are of interest. The report is particularly concerned that general practitioners should be more involved in the child abuse system (see pages 235-238) and that solicitors should be expected to attend case conferences where it is thought care proceedings might be a disposal. The findings from this study confirm the view that both the professional groups are rare attenders at case conferences.

12. It is notable that the Beckford Inquiry Report was critical of conferences where the views of a wide range of professionals were not sought. Clearly social workers for many of the reasons already outlined prefer smaller possibly less contentious gatherings. There is obviously a great need to establish guidelines on this which are both effective in terms of child protection, but also workable in practice.

13. These cases were empirical examples of the types of findings made by Giovannoni and Becerra, namely that different professions, often because of occupational interests and responsibilities, give different weight to different types of abuse. In the cases where social workers resisted conferences, they clearly felt that the standards of care within the homes in question were not greatly different from those of the rest of their clients. (Dingwall *et al.*'s 'cultural relativism' at work). Yet the sexual abuse case considered less serious by the police and other agencies was seen by the social worker as of far greater importance. A possible reason for this is the fact that such cases are thought by the social work profession to be a product of dysfunctional family dynamics, an area where social work skills and expertise are seen as particularly relevant.

14. R. Dingwall, (1977), '"Atrocity Stories" and Professional Relationships, *Sociology of Work and Occupations*, Vol. 4, No. 4. 1977.

15. C. Hallett and O. Stevenson, (1980), op. cit.

16. M.A. Lynch and J. Roberts, (1977), 'Predicting child abuse: signs of failure in the maternity hospital', *British Medical Journal*, 1, 624-6.

17. See M. Lynch, J. Roberts and B. Roberts, (1978), 'Predisposing factors within the family', (2) in V. Carver, (ed) *Child Abuse: a study text*, Open University.

18. R. Dingwall *et al.*, (1983), op. cit. (pp. 149-50).

19. R. Dingwall *et al.*, (1983), op. cit. (p. 206).

20. H. Parker, M. Casburn and D. Turnbull, (1981), *Receiving Juvenile Justice*, Blackwell.

21. R. Dingwall *et al.*, (1983), op. cit.

22. T. Brown and J. Waters (ed.) (1985). 'Parental Participation in Case Conferences' B.A.S.P.C.A.N.

Chapter 6

After the Case Conference – Working with Families

It would thus appear that social work practice with children and families has become far more authoritative and decisive and has increasingly come to intervene in ways which can be experienced by families as threats of punishments. Social workers seem to be developing a practice which says to deprived families that they should be able to care for their children without welfare support and that firm, speedy action will follow if they are not able to provide such care adequately.
(Nigel Parton (1985) The Politics of Child Abuse p. 127).

... there was a distinct unwillingness ever to be censorious of the Beckford parent's behaviour, which may be said to be a facet of over-compensation. Indeed, the most favourable interpretation was always put on the behaviour of Morris Beckford and Beverley Lorrington. Second, there was abundant evidence from Ms. Wahlstrom's recorded notes that she invariably interpreted actions as displays of affection and of caring by Beverley and Morris for their children, in spite of past abuse and signs of repetition of abuse.
(The Jasmine Beckford Inquiry Report. p. 216).

Introduction

Following the report of the Jasmine Beckford Inquiry there has been considerable concern about the way in which social workers ensure the safety of children who after an incident of abuse are returned to their parents. The Beckford case was clearly a high risk one. However, in virtually all cases of child abuse there is some element

83

of risk and the main dilemma for social work practitioners in all such situations is how to combine the difficult task of monitoring the health and well-being of children with that of helping families cope with the difficulties which may have caused the abuse to happen in the first place.

The following transcript of a research interview with a team of social workers and a family aide highlights these dilemmas as they perceive them.

Interviewer:	Do you look for bruises or injuries?
SW1:	We don't often find them.
SW2:	If I notice a bruise I normally think, 'Oh, he's been falling over again.' I don't think I go out of my way to look for them.
SW3:	I don't either.
SW4:	I enquire after bruising.
Interviewer:	Do you sit down and say, 'Right, I've noticed there's a bruise and I'd like an explanation for it?'
SW1:	Well, not quite like that, but, yes, straight and to the point.
Interviewer:	Don't the parents of the kids you're involved with know they're on the register?
SW2:	Oh, yes.
Interviewer:	Well surely they'd expect you to . . .
SW2:	I always mention it, but with some people it does increase their anxiety level so much that you've got to be aware of that when you're investigating it.
Interviewer:	How do parents see you?
SW3:	It depends on personality. Some people see that you've got every right to be going in, you know, because a child's on a care order or the at risk register.
SW4:	I don't think many of them see you as a helpful social worker.
SW5:	You buy their affection, I sometimes feel.
Family Aide:	I feel they see me as a helper really, but maybe I've just been fortunate with the families I'm dealing with. They don't see you in the same light as authority even though they realize you're working with the social worker.

The researcher is asking the social workers how they carry out the task of monitoring children deemed to be at risk. Three make it clear that they do not see their role as that of seeking out signs of physical injury. Only one fully accepts responsibility for a monitoring role. The interviewer presses the reasons for this equivocation in the belief that as social workers they are expected to carry out this form of work.

The responses point to the following concerns – 1. keeping families' anxiety levels low 2. the legitimacy of the monitoring function and 3. a professional (and perhaps personal) preference for helping rather than monitoring. This preferred role of helping was considered in Chapter 2 where it was pointed out that in general social workers were more comfortable in situations where clients voluntarily sought help and where more obvious forms of social control or regulation were not present. Yet, ironically, the family aide, who has a more practical helping function is in no doubt that parents see social workers as authority figures despite all their efforts to play down this aspect of their work!

These and other issues will be addressed throughout this chapter. the focus of which is on the six month period of intervention by social workers after the case conference. To date there have been very few accounts of ongoing social work practice carried out by statutory agencies with cases of child abuse. The most authoritative recent study, that of Dingwall *et al.*,[1] focuses on the early stages of intervention only. The other main sources of information about ongoing child abuse cases are the reports of public inquiries[2] and accounts of therapeutic treatment of families where such abuse is suspected.[3] Both provide only limited pictures – the first because they present hindsight views of patently mishandled cases of serious abuse, the second because they are taken from settings which are not typical of those in which the vast majority of child abuse cases are handled. To some extent, therefore, this area of focus is a relatively uncharted one.

Long term social work in general has been the subject of very few studies,[4] the most substantial recent research being that of Sainsbury *et al.*[5] Their study, while not dealing specifically with child abuse cases, does have some relevance in that one of the findings was that over time in many cases a sense of 'aimlessness' develops between clients and social workers. As the authors of this study point out,

> Some social workers appear to lack a consistent practice-theory. The casework we studied started with some kind of agreed (or at least compatible) task-orientation, but then sometimes drifted into a travesty of the diagnostic model, in which service continues indefinitely and on the assumption that warm relationships are all that are needed to bring about improved social functioning (p. 172).

Consideration will be given to whether such practices are to be found in work with child abuse cases.

Social work intervention will be considered under the following headings –

1. assessing cases,
2. developing intervention strategies or methods of working,
3. working with wider systems,
4. reassessing and reviewing cases, and
5. styles of intervention.

Finally a client view of being at the receiving end of intervention will be considered.

Data is derived from two sets of interviews held with the social workers dealing with the 25 cases. The first interviews with social workers were held between 6 and 8 weeks after the initial case conferences and the second interviews were held approximately 4 months later. Interviews with clients took place between 6 and 18 months after the initial case conferences.

Assessing Cases

While, in much of the social work methods literature, assessment is considered to be a crucial stage in intervention,[6] in practice, except where children are taken into care specifically for this purpose,[7] many assessments are not very elaborate or painstakingly constructed.[8] This was true with regard to the child abuse cases in this study. It has already been pointed out that in case conferences little attention was explicitly paid to theorizing on the causes of abuse other than in general terms. Similarly it was rare to find social workers formulating hypotheses after the case conference about the reasons for abuse taking place and planning intervention accordingly.

There were exceptions –

> I had some fairly general social work plans which were that – I mean I had a theory – I don't know if you can call that a plan – that what Barry and Theresa needed if we were going to pull off a good rehabilitation of the children was a lot of mothering and being a good parent to them.

This approach was clearly influenced by the work of the Kempes[8] already referred to. The social worker hypothesized that the parent had had a difficult childhood herself and needed emotional support to be able to provide a warm and secure environment for her own children.

Several other social work assessments were of a similar kind. However, they were even less specific as to causes and tended to see parents as being 'poor' or 'inadequate' people who could be helped only by a supportive non-critical approach. Several social workers pointed to the need to gain trust and develop relationships with parents in order to be able to help in any constructive way.

On the whole, however, there was little evidence of formal assessments of families taking place after case conferences. Apart from a general tendency on the part of social workers not to theorize, there were several other factors that may have accounted for this. Firstly, in some cases it was clear that the case conference itself was seen as having an 'assessment' function in that, albeit in a rough and ready way, it sorted out cases in terms of risks and to that extent determined general courses of action. Secondly, several of the cases which were the subject of case conferences were already being worked with by social workers at the time and as a result a fresh assessment was not always considered necessary. Indeed in some cases social workers were resistant to the idea of re-assessing situations, refusing to be influenced by the fact that a child abuse case conference and taken place. In these cases social workers showed a determination to continue with the work, largely defined as 'preventive', in which they had previously been engaged. Thirdly, the period immediately after the case conferences was in some cases still one of conflict and confusion and in such instances social workers were often merely reacting to events. A fourth and over-riding factor was the continuing element of doubt in many cases as to whether abuse had actually taken place or not.

Developing Intervention Strategies or Methods of Working

Just as there were few indications of explicit assessment of families, similarly there was little evidence of formal plans of action. The most commonly referred to approaches with regard to children remaining in their own homes were a) building up relationships and b) keeping an eye on things. In a few cases, specialist resources were sought, such as the help of a psychologist or a play therapist to provide specialist services, and in one case in particular which will be examined more closely later a detailed plan for monitoring a child at home was initiated. Again, however, these cases were the exceptions.

Nevertheless, it was possible to gain a clearer picture of implicit strategies from the content of interviews with social workers. Home visiting was the main means of intervention. In nearly all cases there was a period of very frequent visiting around the time of the case conference.

Table 6.1 gives the frequency of social work visiting as reported by the social workers themselves. It should be noted that these figures are an estimated average. At crisis periods i.e. after the initial investigation and at any subsequent allegations visiting was more frequent than these figures suggest.

Over half the cases were visited at least fortnightly which is a relatively high frequency compared with visiting rates of local authority social workers to statutory cases in general.[10]

Table 6.2 gives an overview of the activities described by social

Table 6.1   Estimated frequency of visiting during the six month period following case conferences

1. More than once a week.	7
2. Weekly.	5
3. Fortnightly.	5
4. Monthly.	3
5. Bi-monthly.	3
6. No visits after six weeks.	2
	25

Table 6.2   Social work activities in the first 6 months of intervention

Activities	Numbers of mentions
Financial/material help	10
Casework help	14
(a) Psychodynamic casework	(9)
(b) Social skills	(3)
(c) Marital casework	(2)
General Supportive work	16
Monitoring/Checking for injuries	7
Total	47

workers when discussing their work with the 25 child abuse cases. Most focused on aspects of help to clients. As can be seen only 7 references were made to the task of checking for injuries or other evidence of abuse.

Financial/material aid

Eleven social workers referred to financial or material aid – of these, most were concerned with liaison with the supplementary benefits office or the fuel boards. Two tried to press for housing moves for their clients who were living in crowded or unsuitable conditions. Only one used funds under section 1 of the 1980 Child Care Act to alleviate temporary financial distress. Material hardship was experienced by most of the clients in the study, but many social workers did not focus particularly on these aspects as potential sources of stress which might increase the likelihood of child abuse. Practical aid was sometimes seen as a means to an end i.e. the establishment of a relationship between social worker and client which would then help improve the quality of the parent/child relationship. In other cases it was seen as a rational response to a specific problem i.e. the provision of a fireguard in a case where a toddler had allegedly suffered burns as a result of grabbing hold of an unguarded gas fire. In general social workers were responsive to requests for help with practical and material resources but did not particularly emphasize them.

Casework Help

Fourteen social workers mentioned concerns about the emotional life of individuals and the help they could offer them. They were far more enthusiastic about this type of help than they were about the provision of material or financial aid. This is not surprising given the emphasis still placed on such work by the social work profession despite greater attention being paid recently to broader more socially-based approaches.[11]

Psychodynamic casework

The social worker in the following quote saw her role as syphoning off or ventilating the emotional anger felt by one young mother –

> V. is very volatile and loses her temper quickly – she was very upset one day and she came down, had a good cry, a cup of tea and a bit of a talk – a lot of her problems in the past came out during this and she

said, 'Oh, it's such a relief to be able to come somewhere and talk without interference from family', and we kept it up like that. If she felt things were getting on top of her, instead of arguing with her husband she'd come down and see me.

Another tried to encourage a mother who was continually leaving her eight year old child alone to develop some insight into why she might be doing this –

We had a talk about her relationship with her parents and how she felt her father had been too strict. Maybe this was why she was overlax with her own child. I agreed with her that it is difficult to know which is the middle-of-the road approach to take without being too strict or appearing not to care, which is the way I feel she comes over to the child.

As a general comment it seemed that in several cases the use of casework was somewhat opportunistic i.e. as the occasion arose the social worker would use it to make a point. It is questionable whether such an approach has a great deal of effect. In addition, it may be very difficult for clients to view such approaches as helpful particularly if they see social workers as social control figures.

By contrast, one mother received counselling help from a social worker who was not involved in investigating the child abuse allegation. She attended fortnightly for counselling sessions for a two-year period and was very enthusiastic about the way in which it had helped her –

I want to keep it up. When I go to see A, we talk, but I do most of the talking – she listens, but it makes me realize things. I don't know how to explain it. She's just making me think more and realize more about myself.

Few local authority social workers have either the time or the remit to help in this way.

Social Skills

Three social workers referred to child care and household skills as areas of intervention which they tackled, two indirectly by use of a family aide and a school teacher, the third directly using play therapy techniques herself.

Marital Casework

Two social workers involved both parents in an attempt to tackle marital disharmony, one in an informal way, the other more explicitly using her senior social worker as a co-worker –

> What we've done is talk about a number of things – we've even got them to fill in a family portrait form of the sort used in fostering. We got them to fill in one of those so we could see a bit more about them and we talked about their relationship in depth.

However, in many cases male adults in families were not involved in any on-going work, a finding which has been well-documented in other studies of social work practice.[12] Many social workers are happy to work with female members of families only and many men are resistant to being involved, as the following comment from one social worker shows –

> I have tried to draw him in, but he doesn't really respond in any sort of real way. He's always prepared to talk to you, but you don't really get much response.

With regard to personal casework approaches, therefore, the general picture was one of piecemeal application with the occasional exception. This should not be seen as a criticism. It is difficult to envisage local authority social workers engaging in more therapeutic approaches given the nature of their duties and the expectations of their agencies.[13] Use of extraneous sources of therapeutic help would seem to offer a more realistic alternative.

General Supportive Help

Most social workers saw themselves as providing some form of support for families in the face of a wide range of stresses. Support is a somewhat nebulous concept but can essentially be seen as an activity which helps people cope with difficult external circumstances. In general social workers talked comfortably about providing support – in most cases it was clear that they were very happy to have opportunities to do this in that it detracted from the surveillance aspect of their work. In some cases social work support for clients was paradoxically concerned with helping them to cope with the rigours of the child abuse system itself – a difficult task indeed! The social worker quoted below had been instrumental in seeking care orders on a family of six children following an incident in which one was severely bruised. Three months after the initial case conference she was supporting the mother, against the views of several other involved workers, in her efforts to get all the children rehabilitated –

My role I find with them is really difficult because I was the one who gave evidence against them at the November hearing and was saying to everybody I want the kids in care. Now I've completely changed. I find it difficult. I don't know how clients find me. They must think I'm up the pole.

In other cases social workers gave support as and when situations arose. One mother was taken to court for supplementary benefit fraud, another sought an injunction against her cohabitee. In these instances social workers used their knowledge of formal organizations to help their clients cope with them. Other forms of support were more personal such as helping mothers cope with feelings of depression, as the following quote illustrates –

At the time we were talking about going to work. She was getting a bit depressed at home. Basically I supported her over this saying yes that would be a good idea if you feel its what you need.

There was considerable variation in practice. Some social workers, despite their social control role, were more prepared to get close to and be supportive of clients than others. Most of these were relatively successful at combining the monitoring and helping roles. In a small number of cases, however, usually those where there was much conflict and a lack of co-operation from parents, social workers adopted a more condemnatory attitude. It is impossible to say whether such attitudes caused the lack of co-operation or vice versa, but such social work responses clearly helped to create an impasse. In such cases social workers had to take a good deal of personal abuse –

He wanted me taken off the case. He said I'd been looking for faults ever since I'd walked into their house and that they'd got no confidence in me and all that I was good for was putting on lip-stick.

This social worker while able to rationally explain the hostility shown towards her found it difficult to respond in an emotionally supportive way. In this case the children were made the subject of care proceedings and placed in foster homes. Most of the ensuing social work activity centred around access visits to the children which were held at the social services department area office because of the volatility of the parents. Frequently the parents arrived for access under the influence of alcohol and, according to the social worker, were abusive. The mother clearly felt that the social worker was not supportive and sought the aid of another social worker from a nearby hospital who, came on the phone and said, 'Well, she doesn't feel you are helping her enough. I felt, well, I'm fed up telling her the right way to go about things. If she's going to get the children back, she's going to have to conform and stay off the drink and drugs...

She saw the hospital social worker as being fooled by the mother in the same way that she had been initially.

I started the same way. I think in a way Deborah had taken me in. I found her a nice respectable girl, well-spoken, quite intelligent. I suppose people meeting me think, 'Oh, this social worker's awful hard'.

Clearly, whatever the merits of the case, this social worker, perhaps in order to protect herself, had adopted a stance that was not perceived as helpful by the client and the experience was a bitter one for all concerned.

Being supportive while at the same time exercising the legitimate control that society has sanctioned creates many difficulties for social workers. It takes a great deal of tolerance and skill to avoid the extremes of being unhelpful and overhelpful.

Monitoring

In cases of suspected child abuse social workers do have the important task of checking for further injuries if children are returned home. This was the situation in 20 of the 25 cases. However, in 13 of these 20 cases social workers said they did not check for signs of abuse. Nine of these cases involved children who had been registered. The remaining four were allocated for further social work without registration. Of the seven cases in which social workers did check for injuries, four were registered and three subject to statutory orders. Two types of reasons were given for not checking for further injuries. Many considered that it was the role of other agencies i.e. health clinics, day nurseries and nursery schools to do this and, therefore, felt that this was not their direct responsibility.

I don't check for marks – it has been done through the health visitor at the clinic. If that didn't happen I would have a surreptitious look.

I don't see that (checking for injuries) as my role. The health visitor is still involved. As I say, she goes to the health clinic regularly and she has a good relationship with her G.P.

A second reason given was that social workers were convinced that re-injury was unlikely to happen.

> I suppose I shouldn't say this, but you get a feel about a family and, actually, both of them are very loving with the children and the children show no signs of fear with them or anything. There's a lot of cuddling and natural coming to and fro.

> It's a low priority case in that I don't think there's much to worry about.

Of the seven cases in which social workers said they were checking for injuries, three involved statutory orders and were considered to be greater risks than the majority of cases. However, the other four seemed on the face of it to be no more 'risky' than the cases in which social workers did not check for injuries. In two cases there was no equivocation about the child protection role –

> Immediately the day after the care order I said that part of my job was obviously that I would be coming and checking on Carol and we agreed that they'd change her nappy when I came and they were happy to do that.

In the other case, referred to earlier, a detailed contract was worked out with the parents of a 5 year old child who was the subject of an interim care order and later a supervision order. In this case the child had on three separate occasions in a brief period been seen with bruising to the face. On each occasion the mother and step-father argued that the bruising had occurred outside the home and the step-father had aggressively accused the school of taking insufficient care to protect the child. The injuries were so suspicious that care proceedings were commenced. However, it was ultimately agreed that the child could stay at home under the following conditions –

(1) that she should remain at the school (the step-father had threatened to remove her)
(2) that she should be taken to and from school by her mother and handed to a teacher and when she's collected, collected from a teacher (in order that it would be clear where any bruising, if any, occurred).
(3) Any suspicious facial bruises should result in the child being taken to hospital.
(4) Weekly medical checks should be made at the hospital.
(5) The social worker should have regular access to the child.
(6) Regular meetings should be held between the parents and the social workers.
(7) The grandparents should see the child daily to confirm that no bruising had occurred.

This contract was signed by the parents who agreed that failure to comply with its conditions would entail the child's removal from home. A time limit was set and an agreement made to review the conditions of the contract then. It should be noted that such a contract had no legal binding *per se* and was enforceable only because a statutory order was in existence. However, it had the merit of clearly communicating to the parents the concerns of the social workers and the conditions needed to safeguard the child while avoiding the need to remove her from home.

In other cases where social workers said they did check for signs of injury or neglect the approach was far less formal and depended on some form of unspoken agreement between client and social worker that the latter was checking. For instance in one case in Smallborough a visit was observed which demonstrated the type of interaction that such monitoring can create. The case involved a woman of forty and her 5 year old daughter. It was a long-standing case in that 2 previous children had been permanently removed from her care as a result of sexual abuse and neglect. The current concern was the state of the home conditions and the fact that the 5 year old had a vaginal infection. The home conditions were indeed poor – there were 4 dogs and 3 cats in the household and the smell inside the house was appalling. The social worker was direct regarding her concerns about the physical state of the house –

Can I see the bedroom?

to which the mother's reply was –

Yes, – I've got nothing to hide – I cleaned them up yesterday.

The social worker looked at the bedrooms and, on returning downstairs, conversation centred around the animals and the mess they created. The mother agreed this was so and said she would take some of them to the R.S.P.C.A. to be put down though this would cost money. The social worker felt there would be no difficulty in providing some financial help for this. The social worker was clearly relieved that in this area the client was prepared to take the initiative. It meant that she did not have to exert her authority by mentioning the possibility of removing the child if things did not improve. With regard to the child's infection the social worker argued that the mother ought to take her later in the evening to be examined by the doctor. Her underlying concern was about sexual abuse, but the reason given was the need to ensure treatment as soon as possible. The mother did not want to take her at that time because a clothes club man was due to call then. She, therefore, decided to resist and said she would take her the next day which would mean informing the school of the reason for her absence. She persuaded the social worker to let the school know on her behalf. It was almost as if she was saying – 'If you make life difficult for me I will make it difficult for you'. Both sides knew exactly what was happening during the visit, but at no point was the actual power situation made explicit. In a later discussion with the social worker concerned, she argued that by this means the dignity of the client was preserved to some extent. There was of course a pay-off for the social worker which was to be able to monitor the situation in a relatively conflict-free way.

As can be seen, therefore, there was considerable variety in the way in which child abuse cases where children remained in their own homes were monitored. In some cases social workers were confident that there was little risk involved and did not monitor closely; in others they relied on other agencies to do this e.g. health visitors, day nurseries. Much of the monitoring that was carried out by social workers was done in an indirect way and in only a small number of cases was such activity done more explicitly and directly. The main factors influencing approaches were legal backing, client compliancy, professional ideology and estimated degrees of risk. The aim of monitoring was, as far as possible, to ensure child protection in a way that was deemed to be least intrusive and hurtful to the families concerned. Whether this was achieved can be considered later when examining client's views.

Working with Wider Systems

In general long-term social work it has been noted that social workers tend to work in relative isolation with their clients, often acting as inter-mediaries between them and the outside world.[14] In child abuse work it was recognized from the Maria Colwell case onwards that other systems need to be closely involved in such work. However, in the 25 cases which figure in this study attempts by social workers to set up formal systems for working with and monitoring families were rare. While at case conferences a wide range of agencies was likely to be involved, in most cases the numbers who worked together after the conference diminished very quickly.

Social workers liaised most commonly with health visitors – in nearly all of the cases involving children of under school age. Fifteen social workers referred to their contacts with health visitors. Of these 8 said their relationships were good, 3 said they were poor and four said they had no contact. In only 5 cases was there evidence of structured ongoing liaison. The following comments provide examples of this –

> I was still not happy about the whole thing really because I was visiting and so was Katie (the health visitor), but we were dealing with the pressures, not the underlying problems. So I went to see her (the H.V.) and we decided we'd try and get some sort of history together just to see if there was some pattern emerging.

> We have a good relationship with the health visitors – regular liaison with them – and they seem to very squarely take a lot of responsibility for certain cases and work on some really very heavy cases. They don't seem to sidetrack away from that.

Of those who said their relationships with health visitors were poor the most frequent complaint was with regard to their over-zealousness as social workers saw it –

> I find the health visitors seem to react more vigorously to small marks and blemishes on children than I do.

Another complaint was that they were not able to cope personally with the pressures of relating to families where abuse was suspected.

> The health visitor believes she shouldn't really be entirely honest with the clients because it might ruin her relationship. She's frightened of the whole thing so she doesn't go.

Overall the contacts with health visitors were very variable with a great deal depending on individual preferences, personalities etc. There is clearly room for improving liaison between the two occupational groups.

Eleven of the children attended day nurseries and social workers relied heavily on these nurseries to carry out the physical monitoring of children considered to be at risk. Again, however, liaison was rarely formalized and there was evidence of conflict and disagreement which hindered good communication. Liaison consisted of the nursery contacting the social worker in the case of a child's absence. Some social workers felt that nursery nurses overreacted to situations –

> I've had a couple of calls from the nursery. They've just interpreted every little hiccough as a reason to refer to me. That's a problem we have.

Another social worker described a rather insensitive response to a family where a child was considered to be at risk –

They arrived at the nursery at 10.05am. For some reason – maybe shortage of staff – they wouldn't let the children into the nursery and the parents were very upset about it. I was quite upset about it myself. They came and they started off on the bounce as if I was going to be against them as well. When they realized I wasn't going to tell them off about being late they really became quite accepting about what had happened. I couldn't do anything about it – the nursery wouldn't take the child – but they'd calmed down and were o.k. about me whereas previously they'd have gone home fuming and Sean (the child) would have been blamed for it.

Both these instances suggest a need for greater communication between social workers and nurseries. Clearly although nurseries do serve an important monitoring function there is ambivalence on the part of some social workers to involve themselves too closely with such places – again suggesting a reluctance with regard to a more formal approach to monitoring. In the second case quoted, the nursery by strict adherence to in-house rules seems to have had no regard for its monitoring role and the risks involved in such a case.

The third most mentioned contact for social workers was the school. Overall 10 cases involved children of over school age – social workers referred to liaison with school teachers and school nurses in six of these cases. In only one case was there ongoing liaison with the school with regard to checking for possible signs of physical abuse. Contact in other cases tended to be minimal and not continued much beyond case conferences.

Liaison with other agencies was largely dependent on the needs of the cases concerned – probation officers were involved in two cases and liaison was said to be good. Residential social workers were worked with closely in two cases involving sexual abuse. There was little evidence of ongoing communication with medical practitioners either from hospitals or in general practice. Liaison with general practitioners was mentioned in only 3 cases and in these cases contact was peripheral. This, together with rare attendance at case conferences already referred to, demonstrates the almost non-existent role played by general practitioners in this sample.[15]

In general, therefore, social work contacts with other agencies were confined to schools, health visitors and nurseries. Social workers carried the main responsibility and in many cases bore this alone. It is very difficult to know whether this 'go-it-alone' approach was the result of social work preference – certainly in some cases social workers saw themselves as the best people to work with families because of their, as they saw it, better understanding of the difficulties faced by poor parents. However, it may be that other agencies were quite prepared to remain relatively uninvolved with what in some cases could prove to be difficult and threatening parents.[16] What does emerge is that it was rare for social workers to make use of a more formal network of monitoring. While in several cases they were prepared to work with schools, nurseries and health visitors there was little evidence of systematic consideration being given to such a form of monitoring in all cases.

There are, apart from these formal systems comprising of health and welfare agencies, two other informal systems that social workers in general consider important in their work with individuals – the extended family and the community. With regard to the former there are some particularly difficult dilemmas to be faced when a case of child abuse occurs. By and large use of relatives is a solution for child placement favoured by social workers if it is considered that a child must be removed from his immediate family. The trauma for the child is reduced and continuing contact with natural parents can often be better maintained in such a situation than that in which foster-parents are used. There are difficulties, however, in that there may be intra-familial rivalries or a relative might be considered less concerned about child protection than a non-relative. Additionally some natural parents do not wish their extended families to be involved and in such cases social workers are ethically obliged to preserve confidentiality unless the circumstances are exceptional. Extended families were involved in eight of the 25 sample cases. In 6 of these the natural parents agreed to or even initiated the contact and so there were no problems over confidentiality. In most of these cases the extended family was used to provide temporary care for the child thus preventing a more traumatic separation for all concerned. As the social worker in one case explained –

> Pam (the mother) was pleased they were with relatives. Its been good because Pam, given her history, wouldn't have visited the children in a foster home that she didn't know. I think she's seeing more of them because they're there than she would normally.

In this case, access to the children was less painful for the natural parent – often in cases of abuse such as this the parents' willingness to visit their children while in care is seen as an indicator of the likelihood of a successful rehabilitation and yet such visits because of shame, stigma and sometimes hostility on the part of the foster parent can result in avoidance and, therefore, a negative assessment. In this case the extended family link led, in the social worker's view, to a fairer assessment of the parent's true feeling for her children.

Of the remaining 17 cases, it was clear that in 7 there was no reason for any such contact or no possibility of it i.e. family relationships had broken down or none existed. In some cases social workers saw the presence of the extended family as exacerbating the problem and were therefore keen to reduce possibilities of contact. For instance, one couple lived with the wife's parents and this provided difficulties for any social work contacts –

> When I went to the house I found I could never get a private interview with them – so I suggested to them that they came over to the office.

In general social workers were reluctant to involve extended family members (unless the client suggested it first) and were quick to stress their clients' rights to confidentiality regardless of other issues. In one case the health visitor informed a mother of one of the parents about a child abuse incident, much to the social worker's disquiet –

> In the end her mother got to know. She went up to see the health visitor and she told her everything, which she shouldn't have done really ... but her mum's being really supportive towards her now.

To some extent the social workers in the study might have pushed harder to involve extended families. In one case the social worker was convinced that a parent's relationship with her mother (with whom she lived) was an influential factor in the latter's drinking which was leading to neglect of the children. However, she refused to allow her mother to be involved in any ongoing work and the social worker, despite having considerable influence with her, agreed not to press her on this matter.

Another relevant issue which created difficulties was that of using extended families as a source of information about the welfare of the children concerned. Again most social workers respected the confidentiality of their clients and did not see themselves as having rights to gain information from extended family members without permission. However, from a child protection point of view such activity can be justified. Interestingly there has been little discussion regarding such issues in the social work literature.

With regard to a community-based approach, in only one case was a family put in touch with a community centre or other community facility. In this case it was felt that a mother could benefit from attendance at a women's group. By and large there were few available facilities. In contrast in two cases social workers felt they were working to protect parents from the immediate community. In one case in which many complaints were made about a mother who had left her children alone social workers worked hard to ensure that she was not victimized – they referred to 'neutralizing the community in respect of her'. Again there are considerable problems facing social workers with regard to work with a community-orientation and preserving the individual confidentiality of clients.[17]

Re-assessing and Reviewing

Formal reviewing of work depended to a large extent firstly on the status of cases and secondly on changes of circumstances requiring changes in plans of action.

Reviews of children in the care of the local authority are required every six months by law. Cases on the child abuse register were required by the agency to be reviewed at least every six months. For other cases there was no stipulation.

Cases where circumstances changed were usually reassessed at case conferences. For instance in one case where care proceedings were recommended at the initial case conference, the case was dismissed in the juvenile court and a second conference was hurriedly convened to discuss alternative plans for protecting the children concerned. In another case children were allowed to return to their mother on the condition that her cohabitee who had ill-treated them, did not continue to live in the same household. Having departed, he did eventually return and a case conference was held to reassess the case in the light of these changed circumstances.

In other cases where there were no agency or statutory requirements and no major changes in circumstances there was no evidence of formal reviews taking place. Most social workers said that they had regular supervision sessions with their immediate superiors and most felt satisfied with this mechanism for discussing cases. In general, therefore, formal reviewing was given low priority. Certainly very few clients were involved in review activities and so were given little sense of the formal structure of social work intervention.

Examination of written reviews for children on the central abuse register showed them to be rather limited in scope and completed in a routinized fashion. The review format required social workers to decide whether children's names should remain on the register and to give justifications for these decisions. Most of the comments observed were of a generalized nature and most were rather pessimistic in tone, as the following extracts demonstrate –

At the present time Martin (the father) is in remand in prison leaving Carol (the mother) alone and virtually unsupported to look after Christopher (the child). Due to her immature personality I think she will find it most difficult to cope with Christopher which may result in a crisis situation.

Mrs M is a lady who tends to have a short fuse and sound off if she feels the pressure mounting e.g. financial pressures or school holidays when the girls are at home, thus the possibility of non accidental injury remains.

There is the continued possibility, despite progress, of risk to children – of an essentially unwitting nature – should their mother experience serious re-occurrence of her alcohol dependence. This degree of risk will continue and diminish with advancing age of the children, but is still a reality.

As will be seen in the next chapter de-registration of children's names rarely took place within a year and in many cases continued for a good deal longer without clear justification. This was partly due to the lack of a purposeful and structured approach to child abuse work in general, and this again was partly due to the effects of working within a climate of fear.

Style of Intervention

To some extent the style of intervention adopted by the social workers in this study will by now be apparent. Many social workers eschewed the role of checking for physical or other forms of abuse and were happy to offer help where and when opportunities arose. This is not to say that they were unaware of dangers and risks in situations, and that they did not carry out this role. They did, but they preferred to do so in an indirect way for the most part, using other agencies such as day nurseries, health clinics and schools for this purpose. However, even with regard to these there was some reluctance to forming explicit networks of surveillance of checking. Therefore, the main approach was one of providing help or support to families and at the same time monitoring their children in an indirect way. Perhaps this approach can best be exemplified by a comment from the chairperson of one of the conferences who was agonizing over whether to register the name of a child who had been struck on the face by her mother –

I hope she (the mother) can see it as a white-list of children, not a black-list of parents.

This style of intervention was less apparent in more serious cases where, for example, statutory orders were in force. However, even with regard to these there was still some reluctance to being explicit about the monitoring role.

As a consequence intervention was of a rather unstructured and amorphous kind. Such a form of practice should not be attributed to incompetence on the part of the social workers. To a large extent they were supported in such an approach by the professional ethos of social work and liberal beliefs about freedom from interference for individuals unless there is a legal or statutory reason for denying them this. An additional factor was the pay-off for social workers themselves in conducting their front-line work. Being inexplicit about their monitoring role was to some extent perceived by them as an aid to operating in this difficult area of work.

The next section looks at how parents perceived being on the receiving end.

The Parents' Views

The 10 sets of clients who were interviewed consisted of 3 whose children were made subjects of care proceedings and 7 whose children's names were placed on the child abuse register. Of these 3 felt positively about the social work help they had received, 2 were unequivocally negative and the rest had mixed ambivalent feelings.

In what follows I will rely heavily on the clients to speak for themselves.

Three mothers spoke of their social workers as friends –

Mrs McIntosh's become like a friend. It's a pity people aren't more understanding of social workers.

Me and Joan have always been like friends. We've never been formal. She's come in, I've made a cup of tea, we've sat and had a laugh or joke. If she did get that (a supervision order) it'd change everything between us because I'd know she was coming and checking up on me. I don't like that.

It's different because Leslie and I are close now. We can speak about anything. I sometimes see her in the pub. Because we're close it's harder.

In these cases social workers offered a warmth that the clients appreciated, but even in these largely positive statements there is a tension about the other face of the social worker – i.e. the child protector.

Others, particularly those where care proceedings were originally instigated, were more aware of a conflict of interests. In response to a question about the reasons why social workers were visiting one parent replied –

> As far as I know its because of the supervision order and as soon as it gets finished with the sooner they can stop coming.

These parents were, on the whole, more hostile towards social workers. One considered the social worker to be 'bossy' and only interested in removing her children from her. Another saw social workers as authority figures who 'never give you anything'.

Some parents were ambivalent about their relationships with social workers –

> I trust the social services but only to a certain extent. Its too complicated – I don't believe everything they say.

> You know like when I said to Tom (the social worker), 'Are you going to keep an eye on me if I have another kid, seeing that Kelly's name's on the list?', that's where I felt I didn't trust them. It made me feel as if I'm not going to have another kid if they're keeping an eye on me. When Tom comes I feel sometimes as if there's no point. I say sometimes to myself – they've helped me and everything but when they start talking about things I feel what the hell it's got to do with you?

> She (the social worker) loves Tina and that. She's the type who if I done her wrong she'd take her off me no matter how much I loved Tina. She does her job good. Sometimes she doesn't speak up when she's supposed to. She never said nothing for me at the case conference.

Another found that the child abuse investigation changed her relationship with her view of her social worker –

> I thought Jill (the social worker) was a friend and I found out only through the court case that when she was supposed to be coming round and having a gab she was going back to her office and writing everything down. I told her things as a friend – if I was thinking of her as a social worker I wouldn't have said half those things to her. It was none of her business. I wanted someone to talk to at the time and she happened to be handy. I didn't know she was going to report it all back.

Most of the families were aware that they were being checked on, but in several cases felt that this had not been made explicit by the social worker.

Well, she came more frequently, more regular because of what had happened to Tina. We knew she was coming more often but I didn't know it was for Tina. I realize now that all the time she's been coming she's been looking at Tina – and she watches to see that she's walking properly. It took over a year for her to tell me why she was really coming which was wrong.

Another knew she was being checked on – the social worker told her so, but, according to the mother, never fully clarified the reasons why. In what follows the mother recounts how she tried to get an explanation from the social worker –

So I said, 'In that case they must think I beat my baby up.' She said, 'No, we don't'. I kept calling it a non-accidental injury.' I said, 'Well, if it's accidental why's he on the at risk register?' I said, 'You must think I've done it'. She said, 'That is all part of the system.' So I said, 'Well, in other words, if he falls or if he had his face cut they're going to look at him and say, "Oh, he's on the register. You beat him up".' She said, 'No.' I said, 'Well, that's the way I feel.' I said, 'Well, anyway, I don't care – I don't care what you do.'

One parent was able to reconcile the care/control dilemma –

Yes, he's really good. I know he comes now mainly to check the kids but also to see how I am and how I'm coping with them and how I'm keeping the flat.

This same parent welcomed the fact that she was under surveillance –

I'm glad in a way that they are watching. I think it keeps me from swinging out at him knowing that next day I've got to take him to the nursery if there are any marks on him. Because I know for a fact that next time he'll get taken off me because I've had that many chances. He will get taken off me – so will the baby and I'll never see him again. I'm aware of that now.

Another parent concurred –

I know I can apply to have them taken off the register. I don't want them taken off. I was embarrassed at first but I found it kept me in line. It helped.

Other parents saw the pressure resulting from the child abuse investigation in a less positive light –

I went into a state of being terrified if they got a knock. If they got a bruise or anything I'd ring up the social services immediately and say so-and-so has a bruise, so-and-so has a mark. Its only now that I've got Eddy as a social worker (new social worker) that I realize I don't have to do this any more.

Most parents knew, therefore, that they were being checked on after the case conference. In some cases they had only come to realise this as a result of factors such as increased visiting etc. In general, however, parents were poorly informed about the formal aspects of the child abuse system. Five of the 10 families interviewed said that they did not realize that their children's names were on the child abuse register. One parent saw a television documentary about the Jasmine Beckford case and as a result asked her social worker if her child's name was on the register –

> I was going mad. I said, 'Am I on that?' She said, 'Yes.' I said, 'You'd better get her off it. I'm not having it. She hasn't been bruised or nothing for over a year. I said we want her off it.'

With regard to informing parents of register decisions, the 1980 DHSS guidelines[18] state the following –

> When a decision has to be made whether or not to inform parents (or those caring for the child) that the child's name has been entered on the register, the child's best interests should be the chief consideration. In most cases parents should be made aware in the course of their contacts with professional workers that it is considered or suspected that their child has been abused and it is recommended that unless in an individual case there are exceptional reasons for not doing so, parents should be informed that it has been decided to place their child's name on the register and should be given the opportunity to discuss and question the decision.

In the cases just referred to it is quite possible that parents were told of the register decision after the case conference and that in this period of crisis they forgot or did not absorb the information. What is more worrying is that little or no reference was made to the register later on. Few parents were able to discuss what they had to do to have their child's name removed from the register – it was not used as an incentive to work on child care practices in any way at all. Similarly, one family was completely unaware of the requirements of a supervision order to which their children were subject. They were under the misapprehension that they had to return to court after three years when it would be decided whether or not supervision should be continued. Overall there seemed to be a lack of clear structure in terms of intervention.

> They never explained what they were going to do – it was me telling them what I wanted.

However, despite the lack of clear communication in some cases and social worker's lack of explicitness about their monitoring function, most clients were aware that this was their most important role. They referred to other helping roles with finances and resources and to casework/support functions –

> He's been trying to straighten me out really. I didn't take too much to the little girl because the father was rejecting her – I was too. When she was 6 months I sort of gave her away to a friend to let her adopt her because I just didn't want to know and he used to come down and talk to me and he'd point out things – he would say you'll by sorry, pressurizing me, trying to make me see sense.

> You could say what you wanted and he gave you a lot of moral support.

> Well, when we have our rows she's more like a marriage guidance counsellor, or a referee. She comes back with me to sort it out. She is very good.

Some were less enthusiastic about social workers' intervention efforts –

> I suppose she's trying to be a bit of a psychiatrist. She's trying to weigh us up to see if we are stable.

In a case of alleged sexual abuse of a junior school age girl by her elder sibling, the mother objected to the way the social worker intervened –

> She used to come and see her and take her in her car for a ride – buy her a chocolate bar or an ice cream. It took her a long time to get over it. I think she was getting reminded of it every time she had to go and see Sally (the social worker) and she didn't like that. She's still getting over it. I dare say if she did want to talk about it we would but she doesn't. I'm not going to bring the subject up because I know it hurts her.

Here we see a clash of ideologies between parent and social worker about how to respond to the child's traumatic experience with the parent somewhat resentful of the social worker's 'taking over' of her child.

The responses of the parents were by no means uniform, but the following factors emerged –

1. Some parents did see social workers as helping them despite their awareness of their social control functions.
2. The monitoring role was perceived as being the main reason for social work involvement despite this aspect of their work being played down by social workers themselves.
3. Half the parents were poorly informed about the way in which they

were perceived by the social workers and their agencies – in particular they were poorly informed about registers.

4. Little effort was made to structure intervention or to set goals and targets to which parents could respond.

5. Overall there was complete dissatisfaction with social work intervention in three out of the 10 families interviewed suggesting that in terms of easing the pains of checking families social workers were relatively successful.

Conclusions

Ongoing social work practice with families where child abuse is suspected is clearly a minefield of problems and dilemmas. First, there is considerable uncertainty in many cases as to whether abuse has occurred and, if so, who is responsible. In many cases – in particular those where there are no statutory orders prevailing – the legitimacy of social work intervention is therefore in some question. This, combined with a preference on the part of many social workers for a helping or supporting role which stems from societal expectations and professional ideology, leads to a confused and confusing form of monitoring on their part. Indeed they actively try to blur the distinctions between helping and monitoring for these very reasons. Clearly, this type of intervention creates difficulties for both clients and social workers.

A major problem is how information passed between social worker and client is used – some times social workers are wearing their helpful/supportive hats and at others their social control helmets, but it is not always clear which they are wearing at different times. The status of relationships is essentially a tenuous and mobile one. On one day the social worker might be working with a mother to sort out electricity arrears and on the next removing her child to hospital with suspected bruising. In many ways unless there is clear communication regarding duties, obligations etc. it is an almost impossible situation for both client and social worker.

It could be argued that this type of intervention despite these problems, is less painful for clients than might be true of a more direct approach. This point of view together with the belief that it ensures continued entry to a home were reasons put forward by several social workers to justify their softly softly approach. However, most clients preferred a more genuine approach and disliked social workers 'not being straight' with them. These responses suggest that the stigma is not removed by this type of approach at all.

In addition, not being direct can lead to missing out on opportunities for change and development. Much greater use could be made of structured approaches to bring about such change. For example, if social workers had been more direct about their reasons for involvement they could then have engaged in discussions with families as to how such involvement could be brought to an end or in the case of a child's name placed on the child abuse register how to achieve its removal. A small number of social workers did operate in this way – however, these were the exceptions not the rule.

At the commencement of this chapter reference was made to other studies of long-term social work practice particularly that of Sainsbury *et al.*[19] which found that in general social workers and clients agreed on the purposes of social work intervention initially but gradually this early agreement dissipated and after a year frequently a sense of aimlessness developed. This was considered to be due to the fact that often the social worker had a hidden agenda over and above the issues shared with clients –

> Thus, for example, worker and family might agree that the purposes of intervention were to alleviate problems associated with poverty or the behaviour of a child, but family-members were not often aware that an additional but undisclosed purpose was to improve a marital relationship or some aspect of a parent–child communication. (p. 171)

A contributory factor to this trend was considered to be the lack of formal review of cases –

> This is a matter which could, we believe, sometimes be resolved by periodic summaries and reassessments, and if these were taken up as joint enterprises with clients, some misconceptions could be cleared up. (p. 172)

Hidden agendas and lack of detailed reviews were similarly found in this study.

Jordan has referred to ongoing social work practice with child abuse cases.[20] His concern is more of a political one namely that social work clients should be treated as fellow citizens not as children. He describes the process whereby parents suspected of child abuse become infantilized recipients of welfare. According to his analysis social workers prefer to avoid facing parents with their real suspicions and 'thus treat them as adults –

> The family can become a case, to be visited in a vague supervisory

way, to check up, for the social worker to cover herself. The danger here is that rather than helping, the social worker can instead become part of the client's nightmare. The situation is never defined; the reason for supervision is never spelt out, the problem is never brought out into the open. (p. 165)

There was a clear tendency for social workers to operate in this way in North City. While there are many structural and interactional difficulties associated with protecting children in their own families there seem to be good reasons, both in terms of values and effectiveness, for social work practice in this field to move towards a more direct and open approach in this field. Some suggestions for achieving this will be made in the final chapter.

Notes

1. R. Dingwall, J. Eekelaar and T. Murray, (1983), *The Protection of Children*, Blackwell.
2. DHSS, (1982), Child Abuse: A Study of Inquiry Reports (1973–81).
3. See for instance –
   W. Reavley and M.T. Gilbert, (1979), 'The Analysis and Treatment of Child Abuse by Behavioural Psychotherapy', *Child Abuse and Neglect* vol. 3, pp. 509–514.
   R. Mcauley, (1980), 'Success and failure in applying behavioural analysis', *Social Work Today*, vol. 11, No. 25 pp. 55–7.
   These studies described behaviour modification approaches. The other main treatment approach used in Great Britain is family therapy – see P. Dale, T. Morrison, M. Davies, P. Noyes and W. Roberts, (1983), 'A family-therapy approach to child abuse: Countering resistance', *Journal of Family Therapy*, vol. 5, 117–143.
   A wider range of approaches is reportedly adopted in the USA. See C.T. Shorkey, (1979), 'A Review of Methods Used in the Treatment of Abusive Parents', *Social Casework*, vol. 24, pp. 360–367.
4. See B. Corby, (1982), 'Theory and Practice in Long Term Social Work: a Case-Study of Practice with Social Services Department Clients', *British Journal of Social Work*, vol. 12, no. 6, pp. 619–638.
   also
   E. Goldberg, R. Warburton, L. Lyons and R. Willmott, (1978) 'Towards Accountability in Social work: Long Term Social Work in an Area Office', *British Journal of Social Work*, vol. 8, no. 3, pp. 253–288.
   and
   J. Mattinson and J. Sinclair, (1979), *Mate and Stalemate: Working with Marital Problems in a Social Services Department*, Blackwell.
5. E. Sainsbury, S. Nixon, D. Phillips, (1982), *Social Work in Focus: Clients and*

Social Workers Perceptions in Long Term Social Work, Routledge & Kegan Paul.

6. Assessment has several different names in social work depending on the method used. The psycho-social method of social work intervention used the terms study and diagnosis. (See F. Hollis, (1964) *Casework: A Psycho-social Process*, Random House Press.) Behaviour modification approaches refer to 'baselining' (See B. Sheldon, (1982) Behaviour Modification in Social Work, Tavistock.) Systems approaches use the terms data collection and assessment. (See A. Pincus and A. Minahan, *Social Practice: Models and Methods*, Peacock, Illinois.)

7. See R. Fuller, (1985), *Issues in the Assessment of Children in Care*, National Children's Bureau.

8. See E. Sainsbury *et al.*, (1982), op. cit. and B. Corby, (1982), op. cit.

9. R.C. and C.H. Kempe, (1978), *Child Abuse*, Fontana.

10. See E. Sainsbury *et al.*, (1982), op. cit. p. 28–31. In this study local authority social workers visited statutory cases once every two and a half weeks on average in the first four months and thereafter once every three weeks up to a year.

11. See for instance the concept of 'social care planning' in the Barclay Report. (NISW (1982) *Social Workers: Their Roles and Tasks*, Bedford Square Press pp. 33–51).

12. J. Mattinson and I. Sinclair, (1979) op. cit.

13. See K. Drews, (1980), 'The Role Conflict of the Child Protective Service Worker: Investigator and Helper', *Child Abuse and Neglect*, vol. 4, no. 4, pp. 247–254 already referred to in Chapter 2.
    and also for an opposing viewpoint
    R.L. Hegar, (1982), 'The Case for Integration of the Investigation and Helper Roles in Child Abuse', *Child Abuse and Neglect*, vol. 6, no. 2, pp. 165–70.

14. See E.M. Goldberg and W. Warburton, (1980), *Ends and Means in Social Work*, Allen & Unwin.

15. The Jasmine Beckford Inquiry Report highlighted a similar lack of involvement on the part of general practitioners in child abuse cases and recommended that they remedy this. (p. 235–238).

16. This is a controversial issue. In the Jasmine Beckford Inquiry Report it was suggested that the health services should have played a more prominent role in the monitoring of Jasmine in her own home. For instance it was suggested that the paediatrician should have been invited to some of the review-type conferences that were held concerning the Beckford family after the 2 children had returned home. However, little attention was paid in the report to the availability of such personnel should they be required to attend all such conferences. Frequently social services departments operate on their own a) because they carry the main statutory responsibility and b) because other agencies see their involvement as peripheral.
    The response to the Jasmine Beckford Inquiry Report from the DHSS has attempted to remedy this situation as far as health services are concerned by recommending that organizational responsibility for child abuse be more obviously shared between health and social services departments.

17. See R. Pinker's note to the Barclay Report (NISW) (1982) op. cit. (Appendix B)

and in particular pp. 254–256.

18. DHSS (1980), 'Child Abuse: Central Register Systems', (LASSL (80)4).
19. E. Sainsbury *et al.*, (1982), op. cit.
20. B. Jordan, (1976), *Freedom and the Welfare State*, Routledge and Kegan Paul.

Chapter 7

What Happens to Abuse Cases: Outcomes after 2 Years

The results of child abuse are less potent for the child's development than class membership. The effects of poverty or lower class membership on children are devastating.

(Elizabeth Elmer (1977)) Fragile Families, Troubled Children)

The abused child needs help himself: he needs assistance in improving his self-concept, in loosening his inhibitions and in learning to enjoy life. He needs help in expressing and acknowledge-ing his feelings about assault, neglect and separation from his parents. It may be necessary for him to live adaptively and to negotiate healthily in a family with parents who have numerous emotional problems themselves. Inasmuch as the parents usually cannot give this help, it must come from someone outside the family.
'Behavioural Observations of Abused Children' Developmental Medicine and Child Neurology, vol. 19, p. 384.

(H. Martin and P. Beezley (1977)).

Introduction

The preceding chapters have focused very much on the style and complexities of social work intervention into child abuse cases. Clearly it is of great importance to examine such issues in order to ensure that systems designed to protect children 'at risk' living in their own families are not more intrusive than is necessary to achieve this goal. However, another pressing concern is that of the effectiveness of such intervention i.e. the extent to which children are protected by the efforts of social workers and social services departments. The general public view seems to be that social work intervention in this area is not effective at all. In the introduction to this book reference was made to the cases of child abuse reported on in the media in 1985 that prima facie pointed to failure on the part of social workers to protect children whom they knew to be at some risk. These cases were all ones of serious abuse that highlighted deficiencies in practice. The cases in this study provide a broader more representative sample of the whole range of work done in the field of child abuse. Consideration of the outcomes of these cases over an extended period of time should offer a more balanced estimate of effectiveness.

The situation in the 25 case-study families was considered at two separate periods – 1. at a point in time six months after the initial abuse investigation and 2. eighteen months later.

The Position after 6 Months

At the six month period children from 5 families were in care living away from their parents. In four cases, all ones of serious abuse, these children had been removed at the time of the initial investigation and had, therefore, remained in substitute care throughout this period. In the other case, a further injury had occurred within the six month period which resulted in the removal of the children from their parents. Two sets of children, who had initially been the subject of care proceedings and removed from home, had by this time been returned to their parents, the courts having decided upon supervision orders. Thirteen sets of children were registered at the six month point in time, 11 having been registered initially, the other two following further instances of abuse. One case was still being visited on a voluntary basis and 4 cases had been closed. In all there had been 5 further incidents of abuse, two of a serious nature.

The Position after 2 Years

At two years the situation was as follows. Six sets of children were in care, including 3 who had been in care throughout the entire period following the initial investigation of abuse. There were no plans to rehabilitate these children to their natural parents. In the 3 other cases there had been further instances of abuse. In 2 of these cases there were no plans to rehabilitate the children at all and a final decision had not been reached in the remaining case. The 2 sets of children who had been made the subjects of the supervision orders were still being monitored at home. A third set had been added following protracted care proceedings. Eight children were still on the child abuse register. Six cases were closed, including all 4 that had been closed at six months. Two families were being visited on a voluntary basis.[1] There had been 7 further instances of abuse, two of a serious nature. Table 7.1 sets out these details in diagrammatic form.

Overall, further injuries occurred in 7 cases. In 3 of these the injuries were of a serious nature. In case 12 a young baby suffered broken ribs; case 17 was diagnosed as failure to thrive as a result of emotional neglect; case 22 was a burn injury. All these children were as a result placed in care followed care proceedings. Injuries in the other cases included bruising and children being left alone.

Typical Cases

In what follows the 25 cases will be categorized according to the way in which they were responded to by social workers and case examples of each category will be considered.

There were four types of case in all –

1. Those where intervention after the initial case conference was minimal. All these cases were closed after six months (or not being visited). There was no known reoccurrence of abuse in any of these cases. Cases 7, 13, 15 and 20 fell into this category. Case 10, although the child's name was placed on the register was *de facto* closed by six months. In two of these cases circumstances within households changed considerably reducing the fear of children continuing to be at risk (13 and 20). In the other three, while there was still some estimated risk the social workers decided early on in their intervention that this was minimal. Their prognoses proved correct over time.

2. Those where concern about children continued to exist over a longer period, but where there were no further known instances of injury or neglect. In most of these social workers felt the need to maintain contact, keeping an eye on families and offering support as and when the opportunity arose. Cases 1, 6, 8, 9, 11, 19 and 25 (seven in all) are included in this category. With hindsight social workers were over-cautious in most of these cases. Only three were deregistered during the two year period of investigation and only one within one year.

Table 7.1   Status of cases after the initial investigation and at six
months and two years later

case no.	decision at the initial conference	interim events	situation 6 mths. later	interim events	situation after 2 yrs.
1.	Register		On register	+	voluntary visits
2.	Register		On register	**	On register
3.	Care proceedings		In care		Sup. order
4.	Care proceedings		In care		In care
5.	Voluntary visits	*	On register	*	On register
6.	Register		On register	+	Closed
7.	Voluntary visits		Closed		Closed
8.	Register		On register		On register
9.	Register		On register	+	Closed
10.	Register		On register		On register
11.	Care Proceedings		On register		On register
12.	Register	!	In care (H.O.T.)	*	In care
13.	Voluntary visits		Closed		Closed
14.	Register	*	On register		On register
15.	Voluntary visits		Closed		Closed
16.	Care proceedings		Sup. order		Sup. order
17.	Voluntary visits	!	On register	!	In care
18.	Voluntary visits		Vol. visits	*	Vol. visits
19.	Register		On register		On register
20.	Voluntary visits		Closed		Closed
21.	Care proceedings		Sup. order		Sup. order
22.	Register	*	On register	!	In care
23.	Care proceedings		In care		In care
24.	In care		In care		In care
25.	Register		On register		On register

*=moderate abuse   +=deregistration   H.O.T.=home on trial.
!=serious abuse

However, it could be argued that the continuing involvement of social
workers did have a deterrent effect.
    3. Those where additional instances of abuse occurred often resulting
in more serious intervention at a later stage. In most of these cases there
was serious concern about the safety of the children from early on, but
for a variety of reasons, such as lack of evidence or being over-optimistic
about the possibilities of improvement, they were not removed from

home after the initial investigation. Cases 2, 5, 12, 14, 17 and 22 could be considered under such a category. In three of these cases (2, 5 and 14) children were not separated from their parents for any length of time (usually only for the periods surrounding the incidents of neglect). These cases were still seen as tolerable risks despite the further abuse incidents. In the other three (12, 17 and 22) the children were ultimately taken into care on a permanent basis in order to offer them protection.

4. Those where there was clear evidence of serious abuse at the time of the initial investigation and care proceedings were started. There were six such cases in all. Three resulted in permanent substitute care placements (4, 23 and 24) and three in rehabilitation to parents under supervision orders (3, 16 and 21). In the latter cases no further known abuse occurred.

An Example of Minimal Intervention

The subject of this case was a 13 month old child, Karen, who had been seen at the day nursery she attended with what appeared to be cigarette burns on her hands. According to the matron of the nursery Karen was an irregular attender and when she asked the mother how the burns had happened she gave no explanation. (Both these factors i.e. poor attendance and offering no explanation were seen as indicators of suspicion that the injuries had been inflicted non-accidentally. A good mother by implication would have ensured regular attendance. She would also have known the reasons for the burns and been able to explain how they happened.) As a result a social worker was summoned to interview the mother. He was told by her that Karen had grabbed the grille of a gas fire, which on he face of it was a plausible explanation. Nevertheless, Karen and her mother were asked to accompany the social worker to the hospital where the child was medically examined and detained pending a case conference.

At the ensuing conference the hospital registrar who had examined Karen stated that the marks on her hands could well have been caused in the way the mother said. Karen was considered to be well looked after apart from these burns. However, she did have some burn scar tissue on her body. This scarring was according to her mother the result of a tea-pot scald. Again this explanation was accepted despite the fact that there was no record of Karen having received medical treatment for this. Further concern was aroused by the health visitor reporting that Karen had burned her hand on an electric iron six months earlier, and the police representative at the conference giving details of an incident two months previously in which Karen had been reported missing only to be found a little later at her grandmother's house.

Despite these scares and alarms it was felt there was no clear evidence of non-accidental injury and it was agreed that the social worker should offer help and support on a voluntary basis.

Social work visits concentrated overtly on practical help such as finding a new nursery place when the family moved home and providing a fire-guard and stair gate to reduce the possibility of further accidents. The social worker was covertly checking the child's health and safety – this role was not made clear to Karen's mother partly because he saw a good relationship as a means of ensuring access and partly because as he came to get to know the mother he became more and more impressed with the care she showed for Karen. The main indicator used by the social worker for this assessment was the fact that Karen was not at all apprehensive about being with her mother. Another factor was the latter's open and cooperative attitude towards him. Gradually the social worker became more and more convinced that Karen really had undergone a series of accidents which he attributed to carelessness on her mother's part. Visiting took place weekly for the first six weeks and thereafter approximately once every six weeks. The case was closed after six months – the health visitor was still statutorily involved and Karen was attending the day nursery. Therefore, indiscreet monitoring would still continue. There had been no further incidents of suspected abuse eighteen months later.

As can be seen the assessment of this case was a very rough and ready affair. At the time of the case conference Karen's mother was given the benefit of some considerable doubt regarding the spate of accidents that had happened to such a young child. The social worker on follow-up visiting came to the conclusion early on that the child and her mother related well. The subject of child abuse was rarely raised and focus was soon placed on providing help and support. In many ways, and this was true also of two other 'minimal intervention' cases, the risk to the child seemed to merit more concern and social work time than was actually given. Nevertheless, with hindsight, the implicit assessment that this was a low-risk case was proved correct by the outcome after two years.

An Example of Extended Social Work Involvement in a
Moderate Risk Case

Mrs. Armstrong had three children, aged 10, 8 and 6. She was a widow living with her own mother and the three children. She had a history of alcoholism dating from the death of her husband several years previously. Her drinking was fairly continuous with occasional heavy bouts that often resulted in criminal offences such as breach of the peace. At the time of the allegation of abuse Mrs. Armstrong had been the subject of a probation order for two years. Her children had been placed in temporary care on several occasions following her drinking bouts and once for a longer period when she had entered a hostel for alcoholics to try and 'kick the habit' – unsuccessfully. Her own mother helped to some extent, but felt unable to care for all the children in Mrs. Armstrong's absence. The incident which prompted the case conference followed another heavy drinking bout. Mrs. Armstrong was apprehended by the police as she was trying to hitch a lift on a motorway. She was very drunk and had her 8 year old daughter with her. Mrs. Armstrong was admitted to a psychiatric hospital and her children were received into care and placed in a foster home. At the case conference several worrying issues were aired –

1. the fact that the children might be suffering emotional damage as a result of their mother's behaviour,
2. that, in addition, as this recent event indicated, they were also likely to be placed in physical danger on occasions.
3. that the prolonged nature of Mrs. Armstrong's alcoholism and the apparent likelihood of little change meant that the children's long term future was bound to be unsettled and fraught with difficulties.

Additional concern was expressed at the fact that Mrs. Armstrong was involved in a lesbian relationship with a married woman. (She was seen as likely to provide a poor parental model for her own children because of this.)

On the positive side was the fact that none of the children were showing behavioural signs of disturbance. At school they were seen as non-problematical children. Furthermore Mrs. Armstrong was said to care for them as evidenced by her concern for their well-being following crises and their obvious fondness for her.

The conference participants were divided in their assessment of the seriousness of this case. There was no evidence of physical abuse and adverse emotional effects on the children as a result of their mother's behaviour were not obvious. Nevertheless voluntary efforts to bring about change had so far proved unsuccessful. A decision was reached, therefore, to initiate care proceedings with a view to obtaining a supervision order in the hope that this would bring home to Mrs. Armstrong the seriousness of the situation and give the local authority greater powers in future dealings with the family.

Ultimately care proceedings were discontinued. The social worker had not been happy about such a course of action in the first place and it was felt that there was little evidence of the kind that would carry much weight in court. The children's names were placed on the child abuse register and social work and probation visits continued as before.

Because the focus had shifted to the protection of the children, the social services department took over the main intervention role. For the first six months visiting took place on a twice-weekly basis. The child protection role was made more explicit than before. However, the social worker who took over the case attached considerable importance to counselling Mrs. Armstrong and over time a relationship of trust and mutual respect developed. Despite this Mrs. Armstrong continued to drink heavily and was also becoming dependent on tranquilisers, but there was no known reoccurrence of physical risk to the children over this period of time.

Eighteen months later Mrs. Armstrong had stopped drinking and had managed to maintain her abstinence for five months. The main impetus had come from her attendance at an evangelical Christian rally and she had also been supported by a local vicar. There can be little doubt that in addition, social work support – she was still being visited by the same social worker about whose backing she was effusively enthusiastic – had contributed to the change. Social work visiting was by this time much less frequent than before and the protection of the children was no longer a reason for concern. The children's names were still on the child abuse register, but the prognosis was a good one.

This case had a successful outcome, whatever the reason. It is not clear whether the social work focus on concerns for the children acted as the 'push' factor for change. Nevertheless, Mrs. Armstrong did feel that the threat of more serious intervention had a stabilizing effect on her behaviour. As mentioned before, in some cases in this category social work intervention was perceived by parents as outstaying its welcome. Such parents saw social work visits after the initial period as being without purpose. It is probable that the social worker in Mrs. Armstrong's case was valued because he was relatively explicit about the child protection role whereas in these other cases social workers were more circumspect about their reasons for continuing intervention.

A Case of Escalating Seriousness

The case to be described was perhaps the least successful of all 25 cases examined, and in some ways has similarities, in type, with the events surrounding the Jasmine Beckford case. It should be pointed out that not all the cases in this category were as serious in terms of ultimate outcome.

This case originated with bruising found on a two year old child, Rachel. The mother, Mrs. Brown, and her cohabitee took the child to the casualty department of one of the children's hospitals with a burn on her arm which they said was a sun burn. On examination the hospital registrar was prepared to accept this explanation, but found bruising on the child's back and face which he suspected to have been inflicted non-accidentally. The mother and her cohabitee offered no explanation for these bruises. Further suspicion was aroused by the latter's aggressive attitude and the discovery that another child of the family had been previously registered. These factors led to an application for a place of safety order and the child being detained in hospital.

At the following case conference it emerged that there had been two investigations into allegations of abuse concerning Rachel's older sister, one seven years previously when her name had been placed on the register and the other two years ago. On both occasions it was suspected that the child's natural father had inflicted bruising. Despite her being on the register, the social services department had ceased all contact until recently when Mrs. Brown had requested help with cooking facilities. The hospital registrar confirmed that the burns on Rachel's arm were likely to have been caused by over-exposure to the sun and the other injuries to have been the result of ill treatment. The police had already interviewed Mrs. Brown's cohabitee who had admitted mistreating the child and had been taken into custody. Rachel's older sister and a third child had, in the meanwhile, been placed with the maternal grandparents. As it seemed that the cohabitee was likely to be off the scene for some time and Mrs. Brown was saying that she would not have him back in the house, it was agreed to let the place of safety orders lapse and to allow the children to return to her. The names of the two children who had not been on the register previously were registered and the social worker agreed to keep a close watch on developments in the household. Neither the police nor the NSPCC inspector were convinced that this was the best course of action in that they considered the mother was not affording sufficient protection to her children.

The social worker maintained close contact for five weeks. It was made clear to Mrs. Brown that if her cohabitee returned to the home the children would be removed immediately. Mrs. Brown was adamant that such a situation would not arise. However, following his trial the cohabitee was made the subject of a probation order and did return to the household. Accordingly all three children were removed on place of safety orders and a second case conference was held. There was considerable disagreement at this conference. The important determining factors were 1) the moderate nature of the injuries and 2) support for working with the family as a whole from the psychiatrist who had examined the cohabitee while he was in custody. This pointed to a decision which would maintain the family as a unit. However, Mrs. Brown had proved to be very uncooperative with the social worker. The outcome was a compromise decision whereby care proceedings were to be initiated with a view to obtaining care orders, but with the proviso that the children would return home-on-trial immediately after the hearing. It was felt that on this basis the hearing was likely to be uncontested and the children would be adequately protected. It was predicted that a contested hearing would result only in the making of supervision orders which were considered to be insufficient to provide the protection the children needed. This course of action was adopted. Care orders were obtained and the children returned to the care of Mrs. Brown and her cohabitee.

In the period following the court hearing the social worker visited twice a week. Her child protection role was made clear, but the main focus of her visits was to assist the parents to improve their child care skills. Little headway was made with the cohabitee in this respect and in practice the probation officer worked with him and the social worker with Mrs. Brown. During this period there was a good deal of domestic disturbance and conflict between the two. Five months after the initial case conference Mrs. Brown gave birth to a baby daughter. The social worker had made some plans for this insisting that in the period around the birth the three children should live with the maternal grandparents again and that a case conference should be held to reassess the situation in the light of the new arrival. This was duly done. At this case conference there was considerable unease regarding the new baby's future. There were accounts from the probation officer of the cohabitee shouting at the baby and concern because he had made it clear that he wanted a boy not a girl. However, it was decided to continue monitoring the situation in the hope that with just the parents and the baby in the home (the other children were to remain temporarily with their grandparents) some form of bonding or unity was more likely to develop. This proved to be disastrously wrong. One month later the baby suffered eight fractures to the ribs, the cohabitee was charged, later convicted and sent to prison. The baby was made the subject of a care order soon afterwards. A month later she was returned to Mrs. Brown on a home-on-trial basis, an agreement having been reached whereby she looked after two of the children (including the baby) while her parents looked after the other two. Mrs. Brown was now living alone and likely to do so for the foreseeable future. Social work visiting continued as before. Both the under school age children attended a nursery on a daily basis and the situation remained relatively stable for a period of nine months. At this time further unexplained bruising was found on the youngest child. The standard of care generally provided by Mrs. Brown was very poor. By two years after the initial case conference the two children in her care had been removed and decisions were about to be taken regarding their long-term future.

This was a case where, unlike that of Jasmine Beckford, the social services department was acutely aware of the fact that children were at risk. According to a report about this case from the area officer to the deputy director 'The fact remains that we were extremely aware of the risks and the case was extensively monitored... This was not one of those cases where this could be said to be because of matters going by default, or unprofessional/dangerous risks being taken.' Nevertheless, one could argue that excessive concern over bonding and support for the mother who had not herself inflicted the injuries did place her children at serious risk. Only after several instances of ill-treatment were the children adequately protected.

This pattern, though with less serious consequences, took place in two other cases. Difficulties in assessing risk and an over-optimistic view of potential for change, possibly aligned with pessimistic views of the advantages of substitute care, led to only gradual realization of the need for greater protection being provided. While at the two year stage final decisions had not been reached about these children's futures permanent substitute care was the most likely outcome.

In the other cases in this category neglect/ill treatment, though reoccurring, was of a less serious nature and at the two year stage it was likely that with ongoing social work and other forms of intervention the children concerned would remain in relative safety with their parents.

A case example of the early use of permanent substitute care

This case concerned 2 children aged 18 months and 2½ years at the time of the abuse investigation. A neighbour reported concern about the care of these children. She described an emaciated child who spent most of his day immobile in a cot. Health visitors to whom the allegation was made tried unsuccessfully to gain access to the house and then reported their concerns to the social services department. Social workers with the help of the police eventually gained access. They found the children, particularly the younger one, in an extremely poor state of health and removed them on place of safety orders to hospital.

At the ensuing conference it emerged that social workers had previously visited the family in response to allegations of child mistreatment. This had been two years before when there was only one child. On investigation she had seemed physically well and reasonably cared for and no further contact was made. Health visitors had found access to the family continuously difficult. The consultant paediatrician who had carried out examinations on the children described the younger child as being unable to crawl or stand and as showing symptoms of 'frozen watchfulness'.[2] Both children were said to be extremely thin, but had gained weight since admission to hospital. She considered the younger child's behaviour to be consistent with emotional neglect and both children to be physically neglected. There was no disagreement about the need for statutory care proceedings to be initiated. Some agencies, particularly the health visitor wanted a commitment to permanent substitute care at that time, but this was resisted by the conference chairman.

The parents were highly resistant to any form of social work intervention. The children remained in hospital for two months and were then placed with short-term foster parents. The parents visited them there on two occasions, but after two months ceased visiting altogether and made no further attempt within the two year period to see them again. The social worker involved wrote to the parents to encourage contact at this early stage. However, no further efforts were made in this direction and the children were eventually placed with long-term foster parents. Social work focus was placed on finding suitable substitute parents and ensuring access for maternal grandmother who maintained an ongoing interest.

Clearly in this case the parental response helped determine and facilitate the decision to provide permanent substitute care. In one of the other two similar cases there was more conflict with parents who maintained their interest, but where the same decision was reached.

A case exemplifying the use of supervision orders in child abuse work

There were three cases in which supervision orders were the outcome of care proceedings. In none of these cases were there any further injuries after the children returned home. It has been argued that supervision orders do not give social services departments sufficient powers to ensure the protection of children and there are moves afoot to strengthen supervision order requirements.[3] Much depends on social work style in the use of such orders. The cases in this study suggest that supervision orders do increase the legitimacy of the social work role *vis-a-vis* inspections of children and can play some part in ensuring their protection.

This case example involved a six year old girl who had received several bruises to the face. Similar bruising had been found on her two months previously. Her mother and step-father alleged that this bruising had occurred in school and the recent bruising while she was being looked after by relatives. The child was detained in hospital.

A case conference was convened. The hospital doctor described a suspicious circular bruise on the child's stomach and concluded that the marks on her face were finger bruising consistent with being grabbed by an adult hand. It was agreed that care proceedings should be initiated. Meanwhile the child was placed with her grandparents on a place-of-safety order.

The step-father reacted angrily to this decision. He abducted the child from school on two occasions, verbally threatened social workers and took an overdose of sleeping tablets. The social services department persisted with the care proceedings and after much consultation decided to recommend a supervision order despite the step-father's behaviour. The court made a supervision order in respect of the child and she returned home. A contract was drawn up (referred to in detail in Chapter 6) making explicit the terms of the order and the steps that would be taken to monitor the child's physical well-being.

Visiting was initially carried out on a weekly basis, then fortnightly after three months and monthly by the end of six months. The parents undertook to have the child medically examined every week. Attempts were made to work with the parents to discuss family problems. These were largely resisted. However, they complied closely with the monitoring aspects of the contract. Little progress was made as to the causation of the injuries despite the social workers' efforts to explore this. At two years after the initial investigation the family was still being visited but no further injuries had occurred.

Conclusion

In general terms social work intervention into the 25 cases over two years was conscientiously carried out. Some cases seemed to have been closed rather suddenly, though there was no reoccurrence of abuse in any of them. In other cases social work intervention seemed to have been over-cautious with social workers still in close contact after two years despite no further abuse taking place in the meanwhile. The purposes of such involvement was not always clear and in some cases children's names were retained on the child abuse register without an obvious reason. Certainly in most cases social workers were aware of risks and while in many cases they were less than happy with their roles as monitors of children and approached this in an indirect manner they nevertheless maintained some vigilance and were acutely conscious of the dangers, both for themselves and their clients, of not doing so. There was evidence of determination to take firm action to protect children and also equivocation in some cases where as a result further injuries took place.

Determining the degree to which risks should be taken in order to keep families intact despite evidence of poor parenting, abuse and neglect is a highly problematical activity. What is clear is that in 18 of these 25 cases of varying degrees of seriousness and suspicion children remained free of further incidents of abuse and in three cases serious abuse occurred while social workers were monitoring and only then was a firmer more child protection oriented response adopted.

Judgement of whether such intervention was effective depends on the purposes of a child abuse system and, as has been constantly argued, these are often contradictory requiring child protection without undermining the role of the family. However, it should be clear from this study's findings that the image of incompetence and naivete summoned up by the events surrounding the Jasmine Beckford case and others which have been publicly inquired into is not truly representative of the whole range of child abuse work carried out by social workers and others involved in this field. At the same time consideration of these cases suggests that what happened in Jasmine Beckford's case was not a one-off catastrophe, but an example of all the worst aspects of practice lumped together in one case. There is an obvious need for improvement in practice, but this needs to be carried out realistically in the light of what we know from a wider sample of work. The danger in using disaster cases as learning tools for all child abuse work is that impossible demands are made of practitioners. Also families where abuse is of a moderate kind and risks are estimated as low are likely to be subject to over-intrusive intervention. While, as has been seen in these case-studies, estimating risks is not easy, some steps can be taken to facilitate this provided the climate of fear is not too oppressive. Some suggestions for such improvements are offered in the final chapter.

Notes

1. One case did not fit into these categories – case 18. Concern about the child in question existed at the initial investigation. However, it was decided to maintain contact on a voluntary basis because of lack of evidence and a good ongoing relationship with the social worker who had known the family for several years. Eighteen months later a further moderate injury occurred. Again it was agreed to continue involvement on a voluntary basis. The family was seen as reasonably secure and the risk to the child was estimated as being no greater than before.
2. For a brief account of this see C. Ounsted, R. Oppenheimer and J. Lindsay, 'Aspects of bonding failure', in C.M. Lee, (1978), *Child Abuse: a reader and sourcebook*, Open University Press.
3. See DHSS, (1985), *A Review of Child Care Law*, HMSO.

Chapter 8

Present and Future

Introduction

This study has looked in detail at three areas of social work intervention into families where abuse/neglect is suspected i.e. the detection/investigation stage, the decision making process and finally ongoing work with families. The sample of families in the study has been representative of the middle to serious end of cases of abuse normally dealt with by child abuse systems. The system depicted is fairly typical of those where the NSPCC do not play a prominent role and was managed by child abuse consultants along the lines recommended by the Beckford inquiry report. At the beginning of this study 5 areas of interest were outlined, namely –

1. How social workers operated within and experienced the child abuse system.
2. How the decision-making process, in particular the case conference, operated.
3. How social workers worked with families where child abuse was suspected.
4. How effective this work was, and, finally
5. How families experienced social work intervention.

The findings regarding these areas of interest will be considered first and the implications of these findings for child abuse policy and practice will be considered later.

128

Experience of the system

Social workers experienced the child abuse system as a whole in a variety of ways. Some accepted it without comment and others were positive about the support it provided in dealing with difficult and complex cases. However there were others who were very critical of its functioning and saw many negative aspects in the system among which the following were most commonly voiced –

a. moderate cases of abuse were responded to in an overreactive way and amplified by the form of investigation that took place.
b. 'safety first' decisions were more likely to be made by groups of professionals who were less involved with the long-term consequences of intervention than if such decision-making was left to social workers themselves.
c. one of the functions of the way the system operated was to act as a managerial check on social workers to ensure they were responding appropriately to allegations of abuse.

Implicit in these views was the fact that child abuse was considered to be only one of a range of problems that many families who came under the system's microscope were experiencing, and that there was a need to respond to all the problems including child abuse, rather than of necessity giving it priority. In order to do this social workers needed a degree of autonomy and flexibility which the system did not afford.

One response was to avoid being involved in the system wherever possible – this was most likely to happen in cases of moderate suspicious abuse where families were already known to departments and being regularly visited. Generally, however, such avoidance was rare because of high risk to the social workers themselves.

Nevertheless, a negative response to the system as a whole pervaded and created dysfunctional effects with regard to its formal aims. The most obvious of these were 1) a high degree of wariness within the case conference setting and 2) an overprotectiveness towards clients in their monitoring of cases afterwards. Wishing to spare their clients the pains of the full impact of the system led later on to problems with communication and confusion about the reasons for visiting.

Decision-making and case conferences

At their worst case conferences were seen by social workers as over-populated uncertain gatherings likely to reach rather unpredictable conclusions about families. At their best they were seen as well co-ordinated responses to complex problems where the responsibility for important decisions regarding the protection of children and the rights of parents could be sensibly shared.

Direct observation of case conferences suggested that most fell between these two extremes. By and large they provided a rough-and-ready assessment of cases, allocating them to one of four available disposals. In the middle range, however, (i.e. decisions to allocate to a social worker for further involvement with or without the child's name being placed on the abuse register) there was considerable uncertainty and few clear criteria for differentiating between these two types of disposal. Yet the consequences were likely to be quite dissimilar in that registered cases were required to be regularly reviewed and stayed 'open' far longer than non-registered cases. As a rational decision-making body the case conference left much to be desired. It served, however, other functions the most apparent of which were –

1. as a symbol of the fact that child abuse was a serious issue and was being responded to as such.
2. as a reminder to all participants of their responsibilities and accountability *vis-a-vis* child abuse.

Ongoing Work with families

Much ongoing work with families where abuse was suspected or proven was officially concerned with monitoring and surveillance of varying degrees. Few social workers, however, saw this as their main function and most preferred to give it a low profile. Most social workers preferred to see themselves as helpers and supporters and a small number attempted to carve out a more overtly therapeutic role. but with limited success. A variety of reasons was suggested for such a response –

1. it was almost impossible for social workers to prevent abuse from happening by direct monitoring i.e. they could not be available 24 hours a day. Therefore, they could see no reason for 'playing at' monitoring.
2. being helpful or supportive ensured access to a family where statutory

powers were not in force and therefore enabled at least some form of surveillance to take place.

3. much monitoring of children took place at day nurseries.

Underlying much of this, however, was an avoidance on the part of some social workers of the more obvious elements of social control, supported to some extent by personal preference, professional ideology and societal expectations. In practice much of the activity of social workers was a mixture of help and surveillance, but with the latter receiving no overt emphasis in most cases. With regard to review and reassessment work it was found that in line with other studies of long-term social work this was given far less priority than initial work and led ultimately to a lack of purposeful intervention in some cases. As a rider it should be added that the lack of clear evidence or acknowledgement of a child having been abused did render overt approaches more problematic than they otherwise might have been. In addition there were few guidelines as to how to conduct such ongoing work.

Effectiveness of Intervention

No systematic measure of effectiveness was used to assess social work intervention. However, in 18 of the 25 cases (including 15 where the children remained with their parents) there was no known reoccurrence of abuse after 2 years. In seven cases abuse did reoccur; in three of these it was of a serious nature. Deciding whether or not such intervention was successful or not depends on the standards applied. At the least this view of a wider range of cases goes some way to dispel the public image of social work incompetence in this sphere, though cynics could argue that many cases in this study sample were ones where it was unlikely that further abuse would result anyway. Such is the problem of defining success in preventive work.

The client view

There is only scanty information regarding the client view of being at the receiving end of child abuse investigations – the exception is the work of bodies such as the Family Rights group which has shown much concern about the neglect of parents' feelings and rights in child abuse cases.[1] While only small numbers were finally involved in this study most parents found initial investigations to be traumatic and stigmatic. Some were dealt with aggressively by the police, in particular, but also by other agencies including social workers. Most felt they received little clear information about what was taking place and what the outcomes could be. There were some exceptions to this – parents who were well prepared for outcomes and reassured as far as possible. The difficulty of such situations for social workers should not be underestimated. In some cases they were suddenly compelled to adopt a more authoritative role where previously they had been working more closely *with* families – the latter experienced this about-turn in some instances as betrayal. In several cases there were instances of open conflict and threats of violence on the part of angry parents. Nevertheless lack of communication was a factor stressed throughout social work intervention by parents, as was the related fact that they would have preferred social workers to be more open about their child protection functions. In line with the findings of Sainsbury[2] families said they were able to accept the open use of authority. Social workers who were perceived as having something to hide were viewed with anger and hostility. Notably some families felt they had benefited from social workers 'keeping an eye' on them and acknowledged this and the investigation procedure they had undergone as important factors in maintaining self-control with their children.

Suggestions for improving the official response to the problem of child abuse

A Note on Prevention

The following suggestions for improving our response to the problem of child abuse are influenced by two factors. First, I adopt the value-position that is mainstream in our liberal–democratic society namely that individuals should be subjected to limited interference from state welfare agencies, while at the same time due regard should be paid to the need to protect children. Secondly, my focus will be a pragmatic and somewhat narrow one, that of adjusting/tuning the system that currently exists in order to achieve these often contradictory aims more effectively. However, it should be pointed out that there are far wider concerns with regard to child abuse work that are not within the direct remit of this book. The focus throughout this study has been on what crisis intervention theorists term secondary intervention[3] i.e. how to cope with problems as they arise. There can be little doubt that, despite arguments to the contrary, much child abuse work carried out by statutory agencies takes place with families that are socially and environmentally relatively deprived. Most of the families in this study were already known to social services departments for child care and other reasons prior to the investigation that was the initial subject of the study. Almost all the parents in this study were unemployed. Many were single parents. Most lived in relatively deprived areas of North City. This is not to say that such parents did not have psychological or emotional problems. In fact, most did. However, far less attention was, by and large, given to these wider environmental issues. Such an approach is of course characteristic of social work in general and there are obvious reasons for this namely that in the face of wider political structures social workers are relatively powerless and their prescribed function is generally to focus on personal issues.[4] However, it is important to bear these external factors in mind when working with child abuse situations. There has been very limited progress with regard to more broadly based preventive work in the field of child abuse in the twelve years since the Maria Colwell report was published, though there has been much in the way of exhortation. For instance, the First Report of the Select Committee on Violence to Families published in 1977[5] made many recommendations regarding preventive work from which I will consider three –

The Health Education Council should consider giving preparation for parenthood a greater priority within its existing resources which have recently been increased by £1 million for 1977–8.

Every effort should be made to ensure adequate facilities for care for the under-fives are generally available throughout the country. Whatever other cuts are made as a result of recent reviews of expenditure there should be no reduction in the number of places available for the under-fives.

Social services departments should be well-known, accessible and welcoming and should provide an open-door policy for worried parents.

None of this advice has been seriously responded to. Pugh and De'Ath[6] point out that

Despite numerous recommendations in reports from the DES and HMI there is no central government policy on family life education and few local authorities have thought about its implications across the curriculum ... Outside the classroom such opportunities are even more limited. (p. 199)

Indeed recent moves by the present Conservative government to ensure that the teaching of sex education takes place within the context of love and marriage may have a constricting effect on an already limited service.[7] In addition ante-natal care is woefully inadequate at the present time.[8] Again the comments of Pugh and De'ath are pertinent as they highlight two glaring deficiencies of ante-natal clinics – firstly, 'their failure to accommodate the at-risk groups' and secondly, the 'increasing dissatisfaction expressed by those who do use them'.[9]

Provision for the under 5's falls far short of the Select Committee's universalist hopes.[10] In North City such provision is readily available once a child has been abused, but almost inaccessible as a preventive resource.

With regard to the role of social services departments, very few parents would approach them for advice and guidance in North City. In practice social workers are viewed with considerable suspicion by certain sectors of the population and have been given the title of 'child-snatchers' in many areas subsuming the role of the old-style NSPCC inspectors.[11] In addition in many areas little or no preventive work of this kind (pre-abuse) is handled by social services departments because of priority being given to statutory cases.

The point of this (as I see it) necessary diversion is to stress the need for a comprehensive preventive approach to child abuse work fully involving health, education and other agencies in devising strategies of advice, guidance and preparation for parenthood. In what follows, however, focus will be placed on improving secondary intervention strategies for dealing with incidents of suspected child abuse. For analytical purposes I will consider the system first and direct social work practice with clients second.

The Child Abuse System

The current framework for dealing with child abuse cases developed as a response to children who had been killed or seriously ill-treated by their parents or guardians while already known to or in the care of local authorities. It has been in existence for over ten years now and has gradually incorporated a wide range of types of abuse of varying degrees of seriousness. While there is room for some variation in practice within this system, the continuing climate of

fear surrounding child abuse practice, fuelled in particular by the
number of cases reported on in 1985, has led to a 'play-safe' approach
and heavy emphasis on strict adherence to the procedures. While in
theory this response to child abuse involves a wide range of
professional workers, in practice, judging from this study, social
workers carry the main responsibility for implementing the
procedures.[12] While child protection is the main aim of the system
the whole enterprise is made extremely complex by the competing
demands that families remain free from unnecessary interference.
The price to be paid for complete protection of children at risk in
their own families is too great for our society to sanction. Therefore,
risks have to be taken in a large number of the cases which come
through the system. What has generally been lacking, however, is an
open discussion of policy and practice which admits that complete
protection is not possible. The following suggestions for change in
the system's operation are made with this in mind.

In detecting and investigating cases of child abuse there should be
greater discretion for social workers to decide whether to process
some cases through the system or not, particularly those which are
prima facie less serious. Such discretion should be made conditional
on having consulted with a child abuse co-ordinator. However,
ultimately the responsibility and accountability for such a decision
should rest with the social worker. There are several reasons for
arguing for this. The first is that there is a danger that individual
responsibility can become submerged in group responsibility.[13]
Greater commitment to a course of action is likely to result from a
sense of personal responsibility. Secondly, there is a great deal of
distrust of the child abuse system on the part of some social workers.
The impression given by these was that they were victims of a
process over which they had little control or say. One reason for this
may be a lack of experience and this will be considered later.
However, another important factor is the issue of responsibility and
power. Many social workers were particularly critical of the fact that
they had responsibility without power. The suggestion put forward
here would go some way towards remedying that without putting
children at greater risk.

It is unlikely that the number of case conferences etc. would
greatly reduce as a result of such a change. However, it would
a) eliminate the sort of case where all agreed there was no real need
for a conference to be held at all and b) give the social worker limited
official power to prevent a conference taking place with regard to a
family he/she was working with if it was felt there was little risk and
it would be to the benefit of the management of the case. As pointed

out this happens unofficially at present because officially such risk taking cannot be seen to take place.

There is a pressing need for case conferences to develop a more systematic and explicit approach to decision-making.[14] As mentioned above child abuse work is very much concerned with risk-taking. It seems that this fact should be made more explicit and that trying to calculate the risks involved in individual cases should become the main function of the conferences. This is not to say that conferences did not consider risks – they did, but this consideration was not systematic in any way. Observation of case conferences suggested that implicitly the following factors carried some weight in the decision-making process –

1. assessment of parental character
2. co-operativeness of parents
3. previous history of child abuse
4. availability of police and medical evidence
5. seriousness of injury
6. age/potential vulnerability of child
7. degree of suspicion surrounding the cause of the injury/neglect

Categories such as these could be considered explicitly in the decision-making process. The list is not exhaustive and it may be that certain categories such as assessment of parental character might be considered to be too subjective to be of use. However, it could prove a useful and productive exercise for agencies to draw up their own lists of categories which could be revised and up-dated after being evaluated for effectiveness. Writers such as Parton[15] have been highly critical of the use of check-lists for predicting potential for abuse whereas the Beckford inquiry report has come out strongly in favour of the use of predictive factors. Clearly great care has to be taken with regard to the weight attached to them, but they should be considered in the decision making process.

At present many child abuse systems seem to operate on a four-tier disposal system i.e. no further action, social worker to monitor, without or with the child's name being placed on the child abuse register and care or wardship proceedings. In what follows a five tier disposal system is suggested with much greater explicit focus on risks to the child.

1. *minimal further action (little or no risk).* This should be decided upon if it is found that abuse has not taken place or the abused child is safe from the perpetrator.

2. *social work help and monitoring (low risk).* This should be decided

upon if the injury/neglect is slight and considered unlikely to reoccur.

3. *social work help and monitoring – high priority (moderate risk).* This should be decided upon if abuse has occurred, there is a possibility of reoccurence but no firm grounds for seeking statutory powers.

4. *Supervision order (acute risk not warranting removal from home).* This should be decided upon where there is evidence of moderate injury and risk of reoccurrence without statutory intervention, but where nevertheless removal from home is not at this stage considered in the child's best interests.

5. *Care order (acute risk warranting removal from home).* This should be decided upon where there is evidence of injury and the likelihood that it will reoccur if the child remains at home despite close monitoring.

It will be noticed that registration does not figure in this scheme. There are many dysfunctions associated with registers (as was pointed out in Chapter 5). There are many reasons for suggesting that they no longer be used.

Firstly, central abuse registers are in practice rarely consulted. Many agencies keep their own records.

Secondly, the criteria for registration are not clear and as was seen in Chapter 5 there can be many inappropriate and dysfunctional reasons for considering registration, such as access to scarce resource.

Thirdly, as a result of these factors, cases which are registered are seen as disproportionately more serious than those which are not. Findings from this study suggest there is little difference in terms of risk between some registered and non-registered cases, but a considerable difference in terms of response from the agency. To that extent the register may be creating a false sense of security.

Fourthly and finally, registers do have a labelling function which could disadvantage families. This is exacerbated by the fact that there are no defined standards of proof required for registration.

Only in the case of schedule one offenders can the case for a central register be fully justified. For the rest, agencies should rely on case-notes and good communication with other agencies.

Just as greater attention needs to be paid to risks, so more consideration should be given to the resources needed to reduce these risks. The main resource available is that of the social worker. It is clear that the greater the degree of risk in a case then the more experienced practitioners should be. The recent BSAW guidelines[16] recommend the need for experienced qualified social workers to undertake child abuse work. It seems that the experience of the social worker should be linked to the degree of risk estimated in each case. Thus a generic social worker should be allocated to a case where there is low risk, whereas more serious risk cases should be allocated to a specialist child care or child abuse social worker. There are several reasons for advocating specialist staff at this level of risk. Child abuse work is stressful and demanding. As has been seen in the chapter on ongoing work with families there can be little doubt that social control issues and the use of authority are to the fore in this type of work and not all social workers are at ease in such a climate. In addition the complexities and pressures of the child abuse system are such that those with only occasional experience of it find it a system within which it is difficult to work in a positive way. The approach suggested here could mean a change of social worker if as a result of a further incident of abuse a case was considered to have moved to a different level of seriousness. This could be difficult for a family though those interviewed in this study indicated a preference for openess on the part of social workers about monitoring and checking on this children. If this were generally the case and open communication about risks and fears could be maintained then a change of worker could be achieved without too much pain or anxiety. It is possible that clients might even feel more secure with a an experienced specialist worker.

With regard to resources other than social workers ideally facilities such as counselling, day nurseries and day centres for families should be available on a universalist basis. There are some dangers in earmarking such resources specifically for families where abuse has occurred. Firstly, such facilities can become stigmatizing and secondly the wider population can be deprived of needed resources because they are kept available for 'abuse' cases only. However, there is a clear need for particular specialist recourses for cases of serious child abuse as well. There were very few such resources for families and social workers in North City. For instance there were no specialist foster parents and limited facilities for parents to accompany their children into care or hospital as part of a treatment plan. Some short-term foster parents in the study proved able to work with natural parents, others found it more difficult. Placements that worked well did so because of good fortune (i.e. the right sort of foster-parent happening to be available) rather than by design. Similarly although parents in some cases were allowed to stay with their children in hospital this was a concession rather than part of a designed plan of intervention. With regard to other specialized resources such as play therapists or family therapists again there was little available and child abuse cases did not receive priority for such help.

In general more consideration should be given to ways in which parents are treated under the child abuse system. Three aspects stand out. The first is the stigmatic way in which some parents are handled by agencies involved in child abuse work. Area review committees could reduce the likelihood of this by encouraging agencies, particularly the police, not to see all child abuse as some form of sadistic activity.[17] Those involved in the early investigation of child abuse should be adequately trained to suppress any anger or hostility they might feel about abuse of children when dealing with the parents. The second concerns communication with parents. There seems to be no reason why parents should not have the right to attend case conferences at least in part and be given an opportunity to put their point of view to the professionals gathered there should they so wish. While, as has been pointed out, there are problematic issues needing further consideration regarding attendance through-out conferences, there are no obvious reasons for not hearing parents' views at some stage. In North City attendance at the end of conferences was a concession not a right and was used mainly just to communicate the decision of the conference and to emphasize the seriousness of the situation. Thirdly, Area Review Committees should emphasize that emergency statutory powers are to be used only if it is necessary to ensure the protection of the child rather than as an automatic response. In North City practice varied between these two poles.

Social Work Practice

As pointed out above the major resource available to most families once the initial investigation has been completed is that of the local authority social worker. The following recommendations are concerned with aspects of their practice.

1. There is a need for social workers to be open and communicate clearly with families about the way in which the child abuse system operates. Social workers should be encouraged to be open with clients about their concerns for their children and the measures that they intend to take to reduce degrees of risk. It could be argued that such an open sharing approach is not appropriate in situations where children are considered to be at some risk. However, there does not seem to me to be a likelihood

of putting a child further at risk by such an approach. Indeed increased understanding of the social worker's concern is likely to prove a good starting point for bringing about some changes or improvements. If it is felt that such openness is likely to further endanger a child's welfare then it is also probable that there is something drastically wrong with the whole strategy of intervention.

2. My second point is closely linked to the first, namely that there should be no equivocation about the social control role i.e. social workers do need to come to terms with their responsibilities and duties *vis-a-vis* children considered at risk. Social workers in this study did by and large achieve this but in some cases only via very circuitous routes.

3. Such a focus on social control issues and the monitoring of children at risk need not preclude social workers from providing help and support as well. However, the two activities need to be clearly differentiated.[18] Social workers need to be clear about the priority given to the 'checking' role and then offer help in other areas. This could prove confusing, but can only be an improvement on some of the convoluted role problems that currently exist. Use of other social workers, volunteers and other specialists could be encouraged to facilitate this though due regard needs to be given to not swamping families with helpers.

4. Social workers do need to develop networks of checks on children in an explicit way which should be communicated to parents, rather than avoided. There are difficulties involved, particularly the dangers of stigmatizing or labelling. Nevertheless, certainly in higher risk cases these dangers are outweighed by the need to keep checks on children. More health checks should be made on children where possible[19] – in cases where there are no statutory obligations on the part of parents efforts could be made to negotiate this as part of a contract. Health clinics need to respond flexibly to requests for such monitoring.

5. The use of contracts should be encouraged and where appropriate ways devised of working with parents to have cases reassessed as lower risk and eventually closed. Techniques drawn from task-centred casework approaches could with some imagination be applied in such cases.[20] Very few of the social workers observed in this study seemed to have either the confidence or the knowledge to work in this more overtly contractual way. While social services department workers in their general work do not employ such approaches to any great extent it is probable that the climate of fear surrounding child abuse acts as a further deterrent to this form of intervention.

6. The issue of confidentiality raises particularly difficult dilemmas. It seems clear that social workers must stress to families that their child protection role means that they cannot guarantee confidentiality with

regard to information they might wish to share with them if it relates to the safety of their child. This, while bound to inhibit the sort of interchange that normally takes place within social work interviews, at least initially, should be communicated as soon as possible to avoid confusion and bitterness later and also because it is an ethical prerequisite except in the most drastic situations.

7. Finally, there is a need for ensuring regular reviews and reassessment of intervention. There is little problem with regard to this if a contractual approach is used initially. However, there is a danger that cases may drift if a clear structure is not imposed. Length of intervention is a problematic issue. Obviously there is a fear that abuse could take place again in a 'closed' case and that might act as a deterrent. However, it is important that a child abuse system should encourage some risk-taking and not allow itself to be clogged up by fear of making mistakes.

Other Issues

Linked to review and reassessment is the issue of evaluation of intervention. This is a major topic in itself.[21] It was pointed out in Chapter 1 that there is a dearth of statistical information regarding child abuse in general. There is a need for this to be remedied in order to enable us to measure and assess the problem as a whole.[22] Much could also be done with regard to evaluation at the specific level of individual case intervention.

These suggestions for change assume that social services departments will maintain their primary role in child abuse work. It should be noted that in some countries (e.g. Holland) the medical profession plays the prominent role in child abuse work and it has been argued that one of the benefits of this approach is that is has a less stigmatic effect than the British system.[23] While this may be true this is a comment on the relative status of the professions rather than on the nature of the problem of child abuse itself. Medicalization of the problem may make it more respectable and personal, but social and environmental reasons for child abuse are arguably equally important. Certainly there are dangers (and evidence) that social workers have paid less attention than they might to the role of the health services in child abuse work (other than with regard to investigation) and there is a need to remedy this. Nevertheless it seems that the social work profession does have the potential for being best-suited to keep the primary role that it now has.

However, there is a need to be more specific about the problems of child abuse. To some extent social work has obtained its role by default. The problem of child abuse has crept up on the profession and aided by the piece-meal development of the child abuse system it has gradually dominated much of its work to the detriment of other clients served by social services departments.[24] The phenomenon has been ill-defined[25], the legal framework within which child abuse has been accommodated is ill-suited to the problem,[26] there has been in many areas an overlap of functions with the NSPCC[27] and confusion as a result. In addition there has been a tentativeness about dealing squarely with the problem on the grounds that we may be experiencing a form of 'moral panic' in a period of economic decline.[28] While there may be some validity in this argument the fact remains that child abuse is currently the most pressing problem facing social services department workers and, therefore has to be addressed directly.

There is a need to remedy some of these faults. Suggestions have been put forward at the front-line level. Behind many of these suggestions is the belief that child abuse must be accepted more squarely as a problem to be tackled. Once this is done then more strategic approaches to it can be adopted. At present all types of abuse, however serious or of whatever kind, are processed through the same system. Much greater emphasis needs to be placed on differentiating between serious abuse, likely to reoccur, and more moderate abuse where risks of further occurrence are slight. Having done this strategies should be adopted accordingly. Calculation of risk should be explicit within forums such as case conferences.

At the broader level there needs to be much more emphasis placed on defining abuse more specifically gathering statistical information to measure the extent of the problem and considering the type of resources required to deal with it. Preventive measures clearly need to be researched into and implemented as well. Certainly more effort should be made to de-stigmatize the problem and the services available when child abuse occurs.

It is hoped that changes of this kind at both levels of intervention would produce a more rational and effective response. At present such changes are unlikely to happen. While there are several important recommendations in the Beckford inquiry report particularly with regard to the handling of serious cases of abuse there are signs that the main response will be to tighten up the system as a whole and treat all suspected and actual abuse situations in the same way. Already it has been reported that Birmingham SSD[29] are to institute spot-checks on children living with their parents who are considered to be at risk – an ethically questionable practice which is also certain to be extremely difficult to implement at the front-line. In addition, an attempt has been made via a private member's bill[30] to limit social services departments' powers to return children to their parents home on-trial where abuse has occurred resulting in care proceedings. Such responses do not seem to be the right way forward.

Notes

1. See for instance J. Tunnard, (1983), 'Kept in the Dark' *Community Care*, no. 460, pp. 23–24 May 12 1983.
2. E. Sainsbury, (1975), *Social Work with Families*, Routledge and Kegan Paul, p. 117. 'Long-term resentment was not increased through the exercise of authority.'
3. See G. Caplan, (1969), *An Approach to Community Mental Health*, Tavistock pp. vii–viii.
4. See P. Halmos, (1978), *The Personal and the Political*, G. Hutchinson.
5. H. C. 329 (1977). First Report from the Select Committee on Violence in the Family, Session 1976-77. Violence to Children vol. report. London HMSO.
6. G. Pugh and E. De'ath, (1984), *The Needs of Parents: Practice and Policy in Parent Education*, Macmillan.
7. This refers to the passage of the recent Education Bill through the House of Lords and the hastily introduced amendment that sex education should encourage pupils 'to have due regard to moral consideration and the value of family life'. See M. Metcalf, (1986), 'Prejudice is not enough'. *Times Educational Supplement*, no. 3650, p. 2 June 13, 1986.
8. See P. Toynbee, (1986), 'The Babies who need not die', The *Guardian* July 7 1986, p. 10. and the report of the Royal College of Physicians.
9. G. Pugh and E. De'Ath, (1984) op. cit. p. 122.
10. Within the public sector the proportion of under 5's attending nursery was only slightly higher in 1984 (15 %) than it was in 1971 (14 %). *Social Trends*, 1986 Edition No. 16 (1986) HMSO.
11. J. Packman, (1975), *The Child's Generation*, Blackwell, refers to a similar phenomenon in the areas she studied.
12. However, the findings of the Beckford inquiry report may shift the emphasis towards a more shared approach between health and social services departments (see p. 299 'The duty on a local authority to co-operate with a health authority should be made more specific, to include the duty to consult').
13. This issue of personal responsibility is a controversial one, particularly following the experiences of the social workers in the Maria Colwell and Jasmine Beckford cases. Diane Lees, the social worker in the former case was subjected to extremely heavy personal criticism and Gunn Wahlstrom, the social worker in the latter case, was dismissed from her post. The resultant effect has been to make social workers ambivalent about accepting personal responsibility for decisions and actions taken. Formally they prefer to accept such decision-making as the collective responsibility of the case conference,

though as has been seen from this study they are critical in some cases of the fact that they do not have more power and influence given their direct responsibility for implementing the decisions. A good example of this dilemma over personal responsibility followed the recent publication of an article in *Community Care* (M. Hollis and D. Howe (1986), 'Child Death: Why Social Workers are Responsible', *Community Care*, no. 614 (June 5th 1986) pp. 20-21). In this article the authors argued that even though the child abuse system made contradictory demands on social workers, this was no reason for disowning moral responsibility for actions taken. Social workers had to accept the risks involved in this work if they took on the job. This provoked an angry response and in the letter columns three weeks later (*Community Care*, no. 617, p. 10) social work practitioners argued that decisions were not made by social workers in isolation but in case conferences and by courts. Clearly this is an area in which there could be much greater clarification and discussion.

14. See B. Corby and C. Mills, (1986), 'Child Abuse Risks and Resources', *British Journal of Social Work*, vol. 16 vol. 5.
15. N. Parton, (1985), *The Politics of Child Abuse*, Macmillan pp. 139-144.
16. British Association of Social Workers, (1985), *The Management of Child Abuse*, p. 33, BASW publications.
17. See M. Payne, (1980), 'Strategies for the management of Stigma through Social Work', *British Journal of Social Work*, vol. 10, no. 4, pp. 443-456 for some useful comments on reducing stigmatic effects.
18. See A.E. Bottoms and W. McWilliams, (1979), 'A Non-Treatment Paradigm for Probation Practice', *British Journal of Social Work*, vol. 9, no. 2, pp. 159-202 in which similar issues are discussed in relation to the probation service.
19. At present the power exists under a supervision order to add to it the requirement that a child or young person shall be periodically medically examined in accordance with arrangements made by his/her supervisor (Magistrates (Children and Young Persons) Rules 1970 section 28(2). However such a requirement is not legally binding on the parent. It is currently being proposed that this be remedied by making supervision order requirements binding upon parents in the future. See DHSS (1985). The Review of Child Care Law. Report to the ministers of an interdepartmental working party. HMSO p. 130. If such proposals are made law in future, medical examination of children under supervision orders will be rendered less problematical.
20. See W. Reid and L. Epstein, (1972), *Task-Centred Casework*, Columbia University Press.
21. For a recent account of the issue of measuring effectiveness in social work practice see E.M. Goldberg and N. Connelly, (eds), (1981), *Evaluative research in Social Care*, Heinemann.
22. See M. Walton, (1986), 'The facts which could transform a national scandal', *Social Work Today*, vol. 17, no. 38. pp. 11-12.
23. R.J. Christopherson in a review of Parton's *The Politics of Child Abuse* in *Social Work Education*, vol. 5, no. 1, Spring 86 p. 37 writes 'In the Netherlands where child abuse is seen very much as a disease, not only is the stigma attached to child abuse much reduced, but there is a great deal more scope for flexibility and for working alongside parents.'

See also

R.J. Christopherson, (1980), 'Child Abuse in Holland', *Community Care*, 10 July, 22–23.

24. See N. Parton, (1981), 'Child Abuse, Social Anxiety and Welfare', *British Journal of Social Work*, pp. 391–414, in particular pp. 409–10 which draw on research into social services departments carried out by Parsloe and Stevenson – DHSS (1978) Social Services Teams: The Practitioners View. HMSO.

25. See J.M. Giovannoni and R.M. Becerra, (1979), *Defining Child Abuse*, Free Press.

26. For a full account of this view see J. Eekelaar, R. Dingwall and T. Murray, (1982), 'Victims or Threats? Children in Care Proceedings', *The Journal of Social Welfare Law*, vol. 15, pp. 68–82.

27. This phenomenon was most apparent in the Darryn Clarke inquiry (DHSS (1979)) 'The Report of the Committee of Inquiry into the Actions of the Authorities and Agencies relating to Darryn James Clarke' See in particular pp. 63–66.

28. This is the main argument put forward by N. Parton, (1981), op. cit. While appreciating the validity of many of the points raised in this article with regard to the social construction of the problem of child abuse nevertheless it has to be recognized that social workers cannot ignore it. Facing it more squarely, but with an awareness of the dangers of labelling and amplification is probably the best way forward. Stan Cohen (1975) 'Its All Right for you to talk: political and sociological manifestos for social work action', in R. Bailey and M. Brake (eds), *Radical Social Work*, Edward Arnold) argued along similar lines when social work was under attack from deviancy theorists.

In fairness to Parton in his recent work (1985 op. cit.) he does address the problems of practice and suggest directions for future child abuse work.

29. This policy was implemented following the court case in which the father of Gemma Hartwell was found guilty of her manslaughter. See *Social Work Today*, Nov. 25, 1985, News p. 3.

30. This private members' bill was sponsored by Dennis Waters, Conservative MP for Westbury. It has not been successful, but gained considerable support early on in its passage. See *Social Work Today*, Dec. 2 1985, News p. 5.

Reports of child deaths during 1985. (taken from the Guardian newspaper.)

1. There were 8 cases reported in the *Guardian* in 1985 where children were abused by their parents or care-takers while social services department social workers or those from voluntary agencies were involved. In 6 of these cases the children died.*

> Jasmine Beckford* (Brent S.S.D.)
> Samantha Waldram (Nottinghamshire S.S.D.)
> Tyra Hendry* (Lambeth S.S.D.)
> Heidi Koseda* (N.S.P.C.C. Hillingdon)
> Jane Oliewicz* (Leeds S.S.D.)
> Charlene Salt* (Oldham S.S.D.)
> Bethan & Nicholas Clemett (S. Glamorgan S.S.D.)
> Gemma Hartwell* (Birmingham S.S.D.)

Another such case was reported in January 1986, that of Andrew Riley (on the child abuse register of Cheshire S.S.D.) who was murdered by his mother.

2. There were 4 other cases of child abuse which received wide publicity, but in which social workers were not involved.

The Kerry Babies inquiry – an inquiry into the deaths of 2 new-born babies in Tralee, Country Kerry, Eire.

Louise Brown – a new-born Down's syndrome baby who was allegedly abducted, but whose father was later tried and convicted of her murder.

Christopher Stock – a Liverpool child who was murdered by his step-father.

Michael Brophy – a 6-year old child alleged to have been ill-treated by his parents and to have suffered eye damage as a result. His father committed suicide during the trial.

3. In addition there were reports on a wide range of child murders/accidental deaths, 3 of which pointed to the possibility of some neglect by public authorities.

Natasha and Michael Hurst, aged 11 and 13, who, along with their mother, died in their home as a result of central heating fumes. Originally it had been thought that they had died of hypothermia.

The deaths of children from a junior school in Stoke Poges while on a school trip to Land's End.

Adrian Wright, a 6 year old boy, who drowned in the lido at Hyde Park while on an outing with day centre workers from Southwark S.S.D.

Several other child deaths – all murders – received widespread press coverage, the most widely publicized of all being the murders of Stacey Kavanagh and Tina Beechook in Rotherhithe and the subsequent charging of Tina's mother for their murder, and that of 3 year old Leoni Keating while on holiday in Suffolk.

Clearly this is only a small sample of the total number of child deaths and incidents of mistreatment which took place in 1985. These were the cases which received national newspaper coverage. However, the overall effect has been to further sensitize the public to child abuse and to highlight the role of social workers who are apparently involved in many more cases than was true in the period before the death of Maria Colwell.

Child Death Statistics

There has been considerable controversy about the number of child deaths resulting from child abuse.

On the basis of their study in Wiltshire in the early 1970s, Baldwin and Oliver estimated that 300 children died annually as a result of child abuse in England & Wales. (J.A. Baldwin and J.E. Oliver (1975) 'Epidemiology and family characteristics of severely abused children', *British Journal of Preventive and Social Medicine*, vol. 29, pp. 205–221). This figure was quoted in the First Report from the Select Committee on Violence in the Family. Session 1976–77. (1977) H.M.S.O.

Peckham and Jobling (C.S. Peckham and M. Jobling, (1975), 'Deaths from non-accidental injuries in childhood', *British Medical journal*, vol. 2, p. 686.) quote the Tunbridge Wells Study Group on Non-Accidental Injury to Children which met in 1973 as putting the child death as a result of abuse figure as high as 700 a year, whereas the official figures were 80. Peckham and Jobling suggested that in many cases the coroners' verdicts avoided the issues.

The controversy has continued. The N.S.P.C.C. monitors child abuse statistical returns from its special units which account for 10 per cent of the child population. These figures are extrapolated to give a national estimate. In its 1984 report (S. Creighton, (1984), *Trends in Child Abuse*, N.S.P.C.C.) the N.S.P.C.C. estimated the number of child deaths per year as a result of child abuse fluctuated between 44 and 64.

However, in the *Guardian* on the 12th. of December 1985 the N.S.P.C.C. was reported as having changed its mind. Its new estimate was that 150–200 deaths were caused in this way each year. This resulted from including statistics regarding children who died in suspicious circumstances as well as those where there was proof that death had occurred as a result of inflicted violence.

The following tables (Table A.1 and A.2) taken from the office of Population, Censuses and Surveys Mortality Statistics should help to clarify some of the difficulties. There are two sets of relevant statistics – 1. those where children have died, but it is not clear whether this is as a result of an inflicted injury or an accident and 2. those cases where it has been established that the injury was purposefully inflicted.

If both sets of figures are taken into account we find that on average 235 children and young persons aged 19 and under have died each year in the ten year period between 1975 and 1984 in situations where violence is known or suspected to have been inflicted by

Table A.1 Child deaths in suspicious circumstances.
Cat. E980–989. Injury undetermined whether accidentally or purposefully inflicted

Age	1975	1976	1977	1978	1979	1980	1981	1982	1983	1984
under 1	9	10	2	11	17	13	25	23	16	11
1–4	12	11	11	3	21	12	24	15	19	22
5–9	12	5	1	5	6	6	15	9	6	5
10–14	10	9	16	16	20	12	27	15	6	8
15–19	62	56	59	64	64	67	140	81	81	72
Total	105	91	89	99	128	110	231	143	128	118

Table A.2 Child deaths as a result of inflicted violence.
Cat. E960–969. Homicide and injury purposefully inflicted by other persons

Age	1975	1976	1977	1978	1979	1980	1981	1982	1983	1984
under 1	33	36	18	29	28	13	10	13	15	9
1–4	30	26	33	38	28	17	6	19	22	23
5–9	12	11	13	14	14	10	10	11	3	9
10–14	11	12	14	11	14	7	4	12	5	9
15–19	45	41	35	47	42	37	10	44	34	25
Total	131	126	113	139	126	84	40	99	79	75

another person. If we take the confirmed cases of inflicted violence only, the number is reduced to 111 per year on average. If we eliminate the comparatively high numbers in the 15–19 category which are not likely to include many intra-familial child abuse cases, and include both sets of figures the numbers drop to 124 cases, or using confirmed cases only, to 75.

It should be noted that the figures do not specify who inflicted the injuries – many of these cases may not have died as a result of intra-familial abuse. It is also interesting to note that the number of child deaths where inflicted violence has been proven is declining, though allowance must be made for the fact that over the same period the 14 and under population declined from 12.9 million to 11.4 million.

The statistics we have available are clearly a very complicated and uncertain means of establishing the size of the problem. Until some more precise method based on a specific definition of what constitutes abuse is established, it is highly contentious a) to even make estimates and b) to use them as evidence of trends.

Case Conferences
Decision Making

Of the 55 conferences observed the disposals were as follows –

1. No further action	3 (5.5 %)
2. Social worker to monitor/help	26 (47.0 %)
3. Case to be registered and monitored	17 (31.0 %)
4. Care Proceedings	9 (16.5 %)
	55 (100 %)

It was difficult to evaluate from general observation why in the middle range some cases were 'registered' and others were not whereas the no further action and care proceedings decisions were more readily understandable.

As a consequence a list of variables was drawn up taken from observation notes of the conferences. The variables were as follows –

1. Verbal mention of unfavourable parental character traits
2. Verbal mention of favourable parental character traits
3. Existence of extended family support
4. Presence of supportive professional at conference (as judged by the observer)
5. Presence of a critical professional at conference (as judged by the observer)
6. Verbal mention that parents were co-operative.
7. Verbal mention that parents were unco-operative
8. Previous child abuse history. (referred to in the conference)
9. Low age of parents mentioned
10. Clear medical evidence supporting abuse hypothesis
11. Clear police evidence supporting abuse hypothesis
12. Previous police record (referred to in the conference)
13. Previous police record of child abuse (referred to in the conference).
14. Injury estimated as moderate

15. Injury estimated as serious
16. Age of child
17. Inadequate parental explanation of injury/neglect mentioned.
18. Reference made to poor family background
19. Reference to extenuating circumstances
20. Parental admission
21. References to poor parenting practices.

With each variable a hypothesis was made that there would be some connection between it and the seriousness of the outcome. Thus it was hypothesized that variables (1), (5), (7), (8), (9), (10), (11), (12), (13), (15), (16), (17), (18), and (21) would be associated with a higher tariff disposal and variables (2), (3), (4), (6), (14) and (19) with a lower tariff disposal. Variable (20), that of parental admission, posed problems – it was not clear whether an admission would result in a 'severe' outcome because it constituted clear evidence of abuse or since it could be interpreted as a sign of parental co-operation in a more lenient disposal.

In fact parental admission was made only in 7 cases, 4 of which were allocated for social work monitoring only. Generally care proceedings were in line with the hypothesis, but there was no clear trend with regard to decisions whether or not to register children.

The strongest correlations were found in the following –

1. The mention of poor character traits was mentioned more often in the cases which were registered than in those which were not.
2. Inadequate parental explanation for any injury was more clearly associated with registered than non-registered cases.
3. References to poor family background were also more clearly associated with registered than non-registered cases.

Weaker support was found for the hypothesis that co-operative parents were likely to be treated more leniently. Otherwise there was little obvious connection between decisions to register and the variables considered more likely to lead to such a decision.

It must be stressed that the numbers are small and no attention was paid to combinations of variables (mainly because of the small numbers). However, this analysis did confirm the observer's impressionistic view that there was a fine and occasionally arbitrary line between decisions to register children and decisions not to.

Index